Contents

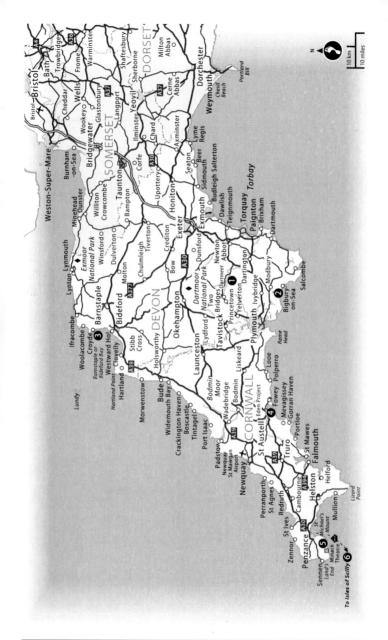

Devon and Cornwall are two consistently delightful regions of England and some of the most popular with visitors in England. Relatively warm and wet, here are some of the place that homesick English people are supposed to see in dreams: the foaming breakers on Devon's rocky coast and the mystical light bathing lonely Cornwall.

In Devon, the natural wildernesses of Dartmoor and Exmoor are sandwiched between a high wooded coastline to the north and the reddish rocks of the Jurassic Coast in the south. Further west, Cornwall entices visitors with some brilliant beaches, headlands and harbour towns before England finally peters out with the subtropical granite rocks that are the Isles of Scilly. Cornwall is also home to the magnificent climate-controlled biospheres in a disused clay pit called the Eden Project, a millennium project that sums up something about the Southwest region as a whole: it's all about the sea, stone and whatever can be done with what's in between.

Planning your trip

Best time to visit England

The weather in England is generally better between May and September, although it can be gloriously hot in April and cold and damp in August. The west of the country is milder and wetter than the east, whilst northern regions and mountainous areas such as the Peninnes are usually the coldest areas.

Transport in England

Compared to the rest of Western Europe, public transport in England can be expensive. Rail, in particular, is pricey compared to many other European countries. Coach travel is cheaper but much slower, and is further hampered by serious traffic problems around London, Manchester and Birmingham. Some areas, such as the Cotswolds, Peak or Lake District, are poorly served by public transport of any kind, and if you plan to spend much time in rural areas, it may be worth hiring a car, especially if you are travelling as a couple or group. A useful website for all national public transport information is **Traveline** ① *T0871-200 2233, www.traveline.info.*

Air

England is a small country, and air travel isn't strictly necessary to get around. However, with traffic a problem around the cities, some of the cheap fares offered by budget airlines may be very attractive. There are good connections between **London** and all the regional airports, although travel from region to region without coming through London is more difficult and expensive. Bear in mind the time and money it will take you to get to the airport (including check in times) when deciding whether flying is really going to be a better deal.

Airport information National Express operates a frequent service between London's main airports. **London Heathrow Airport** ① *16 miles west of London between junctions 3 and 4 on the M4, T0844-335 1801, www.heathrowairport.com,* is the world's busiest international airport and it has five terminals, so when leaving London, it's important to check which terminal to go to before setting out for the airport. To get into central London, the cheapest option is the London Underground Piccadilly Line (50 minutes). The fastest option is **Heathrow Express** ① *T0845-6001515, www.heathrowexpress.com,* taking 15-20 minutes. There is a train service **Heathrow Connect** ① *Heathrow T0845-748 4950, www.heathrow connect.com,* which takes 25 minutes. Coaches to destinations all over the country are run by **National Express** ① *T0871-781 8181, www.national express.com.* There are also buses to Oxford (www.oxfordbus.co.uk), to Reading for trains to Bristol and southwest England (www.railair.com), to Watford for trains to the north of England (www.greenline.co.uk) and to West London (www.tfl.gov.uk). A taxi to central London takes 1 hour and costs £45-£70.

    London Gatwick Airport ① *28 miles south of London, off junction 9 on the M23, T0844-892 03222, www.gatwickairport.com,* has two terminals, North and South, with all the usual

Don't miss...

1 **Struggling up into Wistman's Wood from Dartmeet on Dartmoor,** page 25.
2 **Paddling in the sea at Bigbury-on-Sea and then walk to Burgh Island at low tide,** page 35.
3 **Looking for point break with a surf board at Croyde Bay,** page 50.
4 **Losing yourself in lush vegetation in the Eden Project rainforest biome,** page 71.
5 **Catching a play at the open-air Minack Theatre,** page 83.
6 **Spotting seals, puffins and rare flora on the Isles of Scilly,** page 84.

Numbers relate to the map on page 4.

facilities. To central London, there is the **Gatwick Express** ① *T0845-850 1530, www.gatwickexpress.com, from £17.75 single online,* which takes 30 minutes. **Thameslink** rail services run from King's Cross, Farringdon, Blackfriars and London Bridge stations. Contact **National Rail Enquiries** (T0845-748 4950, www.nationalrail.co.uk) for further information. **EasyBus** (www.easybus.co.uk) is the cheapest option, with prices at £9.99 single, taking just over an hour. A taxi takes a similar time and costs from around £60.

London City Airport ① *Royal Dock, 6 miles (15 mins' drive) east of the City of London, T020-7646 0000, www.londoncityairport.com.* Take the **Docklands Light Railway** (DLR) to Canning Town (7 minutes) for the **Jubilee line** or a connecting shuttle bus service. A taxi into central London will cost around £35.

London Luton Airport ① *30 miles north of central London, 2 miles off the M1 at junction 10, southeast of Luton, Beds, T01582-405100, www.london-luton.co.uk.* Regular **First Capital Connect** trains run to central London; a free shuttle bus service operates between the airport terminal and the station. **Green Line** (www.greenline.co.uk) coaches run to central London, as does **easyBus** (www.easybus.co.uk). **National Express** (www.nationalexpress.com) operate coaches to many destinations. A taxi takes 50 minutes, costing from £70.

Stansted Airport ① *35 miles northeast of London (near Cambridge) by junction 8 of the M11, T0844-335 1803, www.stanstedairport.com.* **Stansted Express** (T0845-600 7245, www.stanstedexpress.com) runs trains to London's Liverpool Street Station (45 minutes, £22.50 single). **EasyBus** (www.easybus.co.uk, from £2), **Terravision** (www.terravision.eu, £9) and **National Express** (www.nationalexpress.com, from £8.50) run to central London (55 minutes to East London, 1 hour 30 minutes to Victoria). A taxi to central London takes around an hour to 1 hour 30 minutes, depending on traffic, and costs around £99.

Manchester International Airport ① *at junction 5 of the M56, T0871-271 0711, www.manchester airport.co.uk.* The airport is well-served by public transport, with trains to and from Manchester Piccadilly as well as direct and connecting services from all over the north of England. **National Express** (www.nationalexpress.com) runs routes covering the whole of the UK. A taxi into the city centre should cost around £20.

Birmingham International Airport (BHX) ① *8 miles east of the city centre at junction 6 on the M42, T0871-222 0072, www.birminghamairport.co.uk.* A taxi into the centre should cost from £25. Several trains per hour run the free 10-minute Air-Rail Link to Birmingham International Station, and other connections across England and Wales can be made by rail or coach, with **National Express** (www.nationalexpress.com).

Rail

National Rail Enquiries ① *T08457-484950, www.nationalrail.co.uk*, are quick and courteous with information on rail services and fares but not always accurate, so double check. They can't book tickets but will provide you with the relevant telephone number. The website, www.thetrainline.co.uk, also shows prices clearly.

Railcards There are a variety of railcards which give discounts on fares for certain groups. Cards are valid for one year and most are available from main stations. You need two passport photos and proof of age or status. A Young Person's Railcard is for those aged 16-25 or full-time students aged 26+ in the UK. Costs £28 for one year and gives 33% discount on most train tickets and some other services (www.16-25railcard.co.uk). A Senior Citizen's Railcard is for those aged over 60, is the same price and offers the same discounts as a Young Person's Railcard (www.senior-railcard.co.uk). A Disabled Person's Railcard costs £20 and gives 33% discount to a disabled person and one other. Pick up an application form from stations and send it to Disabled Person's Railcard Office, PO Box 11631, Laurencekirk AB30 9AA. It may take up to 10 working days to be delivered, so apply in advance (www.disabledpersons-railcard.co.uk). A Family & Friends Railcard costs £28 and gives 33% discount on most tickets for up to four adults travelling together, and 60% discount for up to four children. It's available to buy online as well as in most stations.

Road

Bus and coach Travelling by bus takes longer than the train but is much cheaper. Road links between cities and major towns in England are excellent, but far less frequent in more remote rural areas, and a number of companies offer express coach services day and night. The main operator is **National Express** ① *T08717-818178, www.national express.com*, which has a nationwide network with over 1000 destinations. Tickets can be bought at bus stations, from a huge number of agents throughout the country or online. Sample return fares if booked in advance: London to Manchester (4 hours 35 minutes) £28, London to Cambridge (2 hours 30 mins) £12. **Megabus** ① *T0900-1600 900 (61p a min from BT landlines, calls from other networks may be higher), http://megabus.com*, is a cheaper alternative with a more limited service.

Full-time students, those aged under 25 or over 60 or those registered disabled, can buy a coach card for £10 which is valid for 1 year and gets you a 30% discount on all fares. Children normally travel for half price, but with a Family Card costing £16, two children travel free with two adults. Available to overseas passport holders, the Brit Xplorer Pass offers unlimited travel on all National Express buses. Passes cost from £79 for seven days, £139 for 14 days and £219 for its month-long Rolling Stone pass. They can be bought from major airports and bus terminals.

Car Travelling with your own private transport is the ideal way to explore the country, particularly in areas badly served by public transport. This allows you to cover a lot of ground in a short space of time and to reach remote places. The main disadvantages are rising fuel costs, parking and traffic congestion. The latter is particularly heavy on the M25 which encircles London, the M6 around Birmingham and the M62 around Manchester. The M4 and M5 motorways to the West Country can also become choked at weekends and bank holidays and the roads in Cornwall often resemble a glorified car park during the summer.

Motoring organizations can help with route planning, traffic advice, insurance and breakdown cover. The two main ones are: the **Automobile Association (AA)** ① *T0800-085 2721, emergency number T0800-887766, www.theaa.com*, which offers a year's breakdown cover starting at £38, and the **Royal Automobile Club (RAC)** ① *T0844-273 4341, emergency number T08000-828282, www.rac.co.uk*, which has a year's breakdown cover starting at £31.99. Both have cover for emergency assistance. You can still call the emergency numbers if you're not a member, but you'll have to a pay a large fee.

Vehicle hire
Car hire is expensive and the minimum you can expect to pay is around £100 per week for a small car. Always check and compare conditions, such as mileage limitations, excess payable in the case of an accident, etc. Small, local hire companies often offer better deals than the larger multinationals. Most companies prefer payment with a credit card – some insist on it – otherwise you'll have to leave a large deposit (£100 or more). You need to have had a full driver's licence for at least a year and to be aged between 21 (25 for some companies) and 70.

Bicycle
Cycling is a pleasant if slightly hazardous way to see the country. Although conditions for cyclists are improving, with a growing network of cycle lanes in cities, most other roads do not have designated cycle paths, and cyclists are not allowed on motorways. You can load your bike onto trains, though some restrictions apply during rush hour. See www.ctc.org.uk for information on routes, restrictions and facilities.

Where to stay in England

Accommodation can mean anything from being pampered to within an inch of your life in a country house spa hotel to glamping in a yurt. If you have the money, then the sky is very much the limit in terms of sheer splendour and excess. We have listed top class establishments in this book, with a bias towards those that offer that little bit extra in terms of character.

We have tried to give as broad a selection as possible to cater for all tastes and budgets but if you can't find what you're after, or if someone else has beaten you to the draw, then the tourist information centres (TICs) will help find accommodation for you. Some offices charge a small fee (usually £1) for booking a room, while others ask you to pay a deposit of 10% which is deducted from your first night's bill. Details of town and city TICs are given throughout the guide.

Accommodation will be your greatest expense, particularly if you are travelling on your own. Single rooms are usually more than the cost per person for a double room and sometimes cost the same as two people sharing a double room.

Hotels, guesthouses and B&Bs
Area tourist boards publish accommodation lists that include campsites, hostels, self-catering accommodation, hotels, guesthouses and bed and breakfasts (B&Bs). Places participating in the VisitEngland system will have a plaque displayed outside which

Price codes

Where to stay

££££	over £160		**£££**	£90-160
££	£50-90		**£**	under £50

Prices include taxes and service charge, but not meals. They are based on a double room for one night in high season.

Restaurants

£££	over £30	**££**	£15-30	**£**	under £15

Prices refer to the cost of a two-course meal for one person, without a drink.

shows their grading, determined by a number of stars ranging from one to five. These reflect the level of facilities, as well as the quality of hospitality and service. However, do not assume that a B&B, guesthouse or hotel is no good because it is not listed by the tourist board. They simply don't want to pay to be included in the system, and some of them may offer better value.

Hotels At the top end of the scale there are some fabulously luxurious hotels, some in beautiful locations. Some are converted mansions or castles, and offer a chance to enjoy a taste of aristocratic grandeur and style. At the lower end of the scale, there is often little to choose between cheaper hotels and guesthouses or B&Bs. The latter often offer higher standards of comfort and a more personal service, but many smaller hotels are really just guesthouses, and are often family run and every bit as friendly. Rooms in most mid-range to expensive hotels almost always have bathrooms en suite. Many upmarket hotels offer excellent room-only deals in the low season. An efficient last-minute hotel booking service is www.laterooms.com, which specializes in weekend breaks. Also note that many hotels offer cheaper rates for online booking through agencies such as www.lastminute.com.

Guesthouses Guesthouses are often large, converted family homes with up to five or six rooms. They tend to be slightly more expensive than B&Bs, charging between £30 and £50 per person per night, and though they are often less personal, usually provide better facilities, such as en suite bathroom, TV in each room, free Wi-Fi and private parking. Many guesthouses offer evening meals, though this may have to be requested in advance.

Bed and breakfasts (B&Bs) B&Bs usually provide the cheapest private accommodation. At the bottom end of the scale you can get a bedroom in a private house, a shared bathroom and a huge cooked breakfast from around £25 per person per night. Small B&Bs may only have one or two rooms to let, so it's important to book in advance during the summer season. More upmarket B&Bs, some in handsome period houses, have en suite bathrooms, free Wi-Fi and TVs in each room and usually charge from £35 per person per night.

Hostels

For those travelling on a tight budget, there is a network of hostels offering cheap accommodation in major cities, national parks and other areas of beauty, run by the **Youth Hostel Association (YHA)** ⓘ *T01629-592600, or customer services T0800-0191 700, +44-1629 592700 from outside the UK, www.yha.org.uk*. Membership costs from £14.35 a year and a bed in a dormitory costs from £15 to £25 a night. They offer bunk-bed accommodation in single-sex dormitories or smaller rooms, as well as family rooms, kitchen and laundry facilities. Though some rural hostels are still strict on discipline and impose a 2300 curfew, those in larger towns and cities tend to be more relaxed and doors are closed as late as 0200. Some larger hostels provide breakfasts for around £2.50 and three-course evening meals for £4-5. You should always phone ahead, as many hostels are closed during the day and phone numbers are listed in this guide. Advance booking is recommended at all times, particularly from May to September and on public holidays. Many hostels are closed during the winter. Youth hostel members are entitled to various discounts, including tourist attractions and travel. The YHA also offer budget self-catering bunkhouses with mostly dorm accommodation and some family rooms, which are in more rural locations. Camping barns, camping pods and camping are other options offered by the YHA; see the website for details.

Details of most independent hostels can be found in the *Independent Hostel Guide* (T01629-580427, www.independenthostelguide.co.uk). Independent hostels tend to be more laid-back, with fewer rules and no curfew, and no membership is required. They all have dorms, hot showers and self-catering kitchens, and some have family and double rooms. Some include continental breakfast, or offer cheap breakfasts.

Self-catering accommodation

There are lots of different types of accommodation to choose from, to suit all budgets, ranging from luxury lodges, castles and lighthouses to basic cottages. Expect to pay at least £200-400 per week for a two-bedroom cottage in the winter, rising to £400-1000 in the high season, or more if it's a particularly nice place. A good source of information on self-catering accommodation is the VisitEngland website, www.visitengland.com, and its *VisitEngland Self-catering 2013* guide, which lists many properties and is available to buy from any tourist office and many bookshops, but there are also dozens of excellent websites to browse. Amongst the best websites are: www.cottages4you.co.uk, www.ruralretreats.co.uk and www.ownersdirect.co.uk. If you want to tickle a trout or feed a pet lamb, **Farm Stay UK** (www.farmstay.co.uk) offer over a thousand good value rural places to stay around England, all clearly listed on a clickable map.

More interesting places to stay are offered by the **Landmark Trust** ⓘ *T01628-825925, www.landmarktrust.org.uk*, who rent out renovated historic landmark buildings, from atmospheric castles to cottages, and the **National Trust** ⓘ *T0844-800 2070, www.nationaltrustcottages.co.uk*, who provide a wide variety of different accommodation on their estates. A reputable agent for self-catering cottages is **English Country Cottages** ⓘ *T0845-268 0785, www.english-country-cottages.co.uk*.

Campsites

Campsites vary greatly in quality and level of facilities. Some sites are only open from April to October. See the following sites: www.pitchup.com; www.coolcamping.com, good for finding characterful sites that allow campfires; www.ukcampsite.co.uk, which is the most comprehensive service with thousands of sites, many with pictures and reviews from punters; and www.campingandcaravanningclub.co.uk. The Forestry Commission have campsites on their wooded estates, see www.campingintheforest.com.

Food and drink in England → *For restaurant price codes see box, page 10.*

Food

Only 30 years ago few would have thought to come to England for haute cuisine. Since the 1980s, though, the English have been determinedly shrugging off their reputation for over-boiled cabbage and watery beef. Now cookery shows like Masterchef are the most popular on TV after the soaps, and thanks in part to the wave of celebrity chefs they have created, you can expect a generally high standard of competence in restaurant kitchens. Towns like Padstow in Cornwall have carved reputations for themselves almost solely on the strength of their cuisine.

Pub food has also been transformed in recent years, and now many of them offer ambitious lunchtime and supper menus in so-called gastro pubs. Most parts of the country still boast regional specialities, and Devon and Cornwall are no exception. Both areas have strong culinary traditions. Famous local food include dairy products such as Devonshire and Cornish clotted cream and ice cream, as well as cheese from Cornwall like Cornish Yarg and Brie. Cornish pasties are Cornwall's most well-known food speciality. Seafood in Devon and Cornwall is spankingly fresh, while Newlyn in Cornwall is one of the biggest fishing ports in the UK.

The biggest problem with eating out is the ludicrously limited serving hours in some pubs and hotels, particularly in remoter locations. These places only serve food during restricted hours, generally about 1200-1430 for lunch and 1830-2130 for supper, seemingly ignorant of the eating habits of foreign visitors, or those who would prefer a bit more flexibility during their holiday. In small places especially, it can be difficult finding food outside these enforced times. Places that serve food all day till 2100 or later are restaurants, fast-food outlets and the many chic bistros and café-bars, which can be found not only in the main cities but increasingly in smaller towns. The latter often offer very good value and above-average quality fare.

Drink

Drinking is a national hobby and sometimes a dangerous one at that. **Real ale** – flat, brown beer known as bitter, made with hops – is the national drink, but now struggles to maintain its market share in the face of fierce competition from continental lagers and alcopops. Many small independent breweries are still up and running though, as well as microbreweries attached to individual pubs, which produce far superior ales. **Cider** (fermented apple juice) is also experiencing a resurgence of interest and is a speciality of Somerset. English **wine** is also proving surprisingly resilient: generally it compares favourably with German varieties and many vineyards now offer continental-style sampling sessions.

In many pubs the basic ales are chilled under gas pressure like lagers, but the best ales, such as those from independent breweries, are 'real ales', still fermenting in the cask and served cool but not chilled (around 12°C) under natural pressure from a handpump, electric pump or air pressure fount.

The **pub** is still the traditional place to enjoy a drink: the best are usually freehouses (not tied to a brewery) and feature real log or coal fires in winter, flower-filled gardens for the summer (even in cities occasionally) and most importantly, thriving local custom. Many also offer characterful accommodation and restaurants serving high-quality fare. Pubs are prey to the same market forces as any other business, though, and many a delightful local has recently succumbed to exorbitant property prices or to the bland makeover favoured by the large chains. In 2012, pubs were closing at the rate of 12 a week due to the recession.

Essentials A-Z

Accident and emergency

For police, fire brigade, ambulance and, in certain areas, mountain rescue or coastguard, T999 or T112.

Disabled travellers

Wheelchair users, and blind or partially sighted people are automatically given 34-50% discount on train fares, and those with other disabilities are eligible for the Disabled Person's Railcard, which costs £20 per year and gives a third off most tickets. If you will need assistance at a railway station, call the train company that manages the station you're starting your journey from 24 hours in advance. **Disabled UK** residents can apply to their local councils for a concessionary bus pass. National Express have a helpline for disabled passengers, T08717-818179, to plan journeys and arrange assistance. They also sell a discount coach card for £10 for people with disabilities.

The **English Tourist Board** website, www.visitengland.com, has information on the National Accessible Scheme (NAS) logos to help disabled travellers find the right accommodation for their needs, as well as details of walks that are possible with wheelchairs and the Shopmobility scheme. Many local tourist offices offer accessibility details for their area.

Useful organizations include:
Radar, T020-7250 3222, www.radar.org.uk. A good source of advice and information. It produces an annual National Key Scheme Guide and key for gaining access to over 9000 toilet facilities across the UK.
Tourism for all, T0845-124 9971, www.holidaycare.org.uk, www.tourismfor all.org.uk. An excellent source of information about travel and for identifying accessible accommodation in the UK.

Electricity

The current in Britain is 240V AC. Plugs have 3 square pins and adapters are widely available.

Health

For minor accidents go to the nearest casualty department or an Accident and Emergency (A&E) Unit at a hospital. For other enquiries phone NHS Direct 24 hours (T0845-4647) or visit an NHS walk-in centre. See also individual town and city directories throughout the book for details of local medical services.

Money→ *For up-to-date exhange rates, see www.xe.com.*
The British currency is the pound sterling (£), divided into 100 pence (p). Coins come in denominations of 1p, 2p, 5p, 10p, 20p, 50p, £1 and £2. Banknotes come in denominations of £5, £10, £20 and £50. The last of these is not widely used and may be difficult to change.

Banks and bureaux de change

Banks tend to offer similar exchange rates and are usually the best places to change money and cheques. Outside banking hours you'll have to use a bureau de change, which can be easily found at the airports and train stations and in larger cities. **Thomas Cook** and other major travel agents also operate bureaux de change with reasonable rates. Avoid changing money or cheques in hotels, as the rates are usually poor. Main post offices and branches of **Marks and Spencer** will change cash without charging commission.

Credit cards and ATMs

Most hotels, shops and restaurants accept the major credit cards though some places may charge for using them. Some smaller establishments such as B&Bs may only accept cash.

Currency cards

If you don't want to carry lots of cash, prepaid currency cards allow you to preload money from your bank account, fixed at the day's exchange rate. They look like a credit card or debit card and are issued by specialist money changing companies, such as Travelex and Caxton FX. You can top up and check your balance by phone, online and sometimes by text.

Money transfers

If you need money urgently, the quickest way to have it sent to you is to have it wired to the nearest bank via **Western Union**, T0800-833833, www.westernunion.co.uk, or **MoneyGram**, www.moneygram.com. The Post Office can also arrange a MoneyGram transfer. Charges are on a sliding scale; so it will cost proportionately less to wire out more money. Money can also be wired by **Thomas Cook**, www.thomasexchangeglobal.co.uk, or transferred via a bank draft, but this can take up to a week.

Taxes

Most goods are subject to a Value Added Tax (VAT) of 20%, with the major exception of food and books. VAT is usually already included in the advertised price of goods. Visitors from non-EU countries can save money through shopping at places that offer Tax Free Shopping (also known as the Retail Export Scheme), which allows a refund of VAT on goods that will be taken out of the country. Note that not all shops participate in the scheme and that VAT cannot be reclaimed on hotel bills or other services.

Cost of travelling

England can be an expensive place to visit, and London and the south in particular can eat heavily into your budget. There is budget accommodation available, however, and backpackers will be able to keep their costs down. Fuel is a major expense and won't just cost an arm and a leg but also the limbs of all remaining family members, and public transport – particularly rail travel if not booked in advance – can also be pricey, especially for families. Accommodation and restaurant prices also tend to be higher in more popular destinations and during the busy summer months.

The minimum daily budget required, if you're staying in hostels or camping, cycling or hitching (not recommended), and cooking your own meals, will be around £30 per person per day. If you start using public transport and eating out occasionally that will rise to around £35-40. Those staying in slightly more upmarket B&Bs or guesthouses, eating out every evening at pubs or modest restaurants and visiting tourist attractions can expect to pay around £60 per day. If you also want to hire a car and eat well, then costs will rise considerably to at least £75-80 per person per day. Single travellers will have to pay more than half the cost of a double room, and should budget on spending around 60-70% of what a couple would spend.

Opening hours

Businesses are usually open Mon-Sat 0900-1700. In towns and cities, as well as villages in holiday areas, many shops open on a Sun but they will open later and close earlier. For banks, see above. For TIC opening hours, see the tourist information sections in the relevant cities, towns and villages in the text.

Post

Most post offices are open Mon-Fri 0900 to 1730 and Sat 0900-1230 or 1300. Smaller sub-post offices are closed for an hour at lunch (1300-1400) and many of them operate out of a shop. Stamps can be bought at post offices, but also from many shops. A 1st-class letter weighing up to 100 g to anywhere in the UK costs 60p (a large letter over 240 mm by 165 mm is 90p) and should arrive the following day, while 2nd-class letters weighing up to 100 g cost 50p (69p) and take between 2-4 days. For more information about Royal Mail postal services, call T08457-740740, or visit www.royalmail.com.

Safety

Generally speaking, England is a safe place to visit. English cities have their fair share of crime, but much of it is drug-related and confined to the more deprived peripheral areas. Trust your instincts, and if in doubt, take a taxi.

Telephone → *Country code +44.*

Useful numbers: operator T100; international operator T155; directory enquiries T192; overseas directory enquiries T153. Most public payphones are operated by British Telecom (**BT**) and can be found in towns and cities, though less so in rural areas. Numbers of public phone booths have declined in recent years due to the advent of the mobile phone, so don't rely on being able to find a payphone wherever you go. Calls from BT payphones cost a minimum of 60p, for which you get 30 mins for a local or national call. Calls to non-geographic numbers (eg 0845), mobile phones and others may cost more. Payphones take either coins (10p, 20p, 50p and £1), 50c, 1 or 2 euro coins, credit cards or BT Chargecards, which are available at newsagents and post offices displaying the BT logo. These cards come in denominations of £2, £3, £5 and £10. Some payphones also have facilities for internet, text messaging and emailing.

For most countries (including Europe, USA and Canada) calls are cheapest Mon-Fri between 1800 and 0800 and all day Sat-Sun.

For Australia and New Zealand it's cheapest to call from 1430-1930 and from 2400-0700 every day. However, the cheapest ways to call abroad from England is not via a standard UK landline provider. Calls are free using **Skype** on the internet, or you can route calls from your phone through the internet with **JaJah** (www.jajah.com) or from a mobile using **Rebtel**. Many phone companies offer discounted call rates by calling their access number prior to dialling the number you want, including www.dialabroad.co.uk and www.simply-call.com.

Area codes are not needed if calling from within the same area. Any number prefixed by 0800 or 0500 is free to the caller; 08457 numbers are charged at local rates and 08705 numbers at the national rate.

Time

Greenwich Mean Time (GMT) is used from late Oct to late Mar, after which time the clocks go forward 1 hr to British Summer Time (BST).

Tipping

Tipping in England is at the customer's discretion. In a restaurant you should leave a tip of 10-15% if you are satisfied with the service. If the bill already includes a service charge, which is likely if you are in a large group, you needn't add a further tip. Tipping is not normal in pubs or bars. Taxi drivers may expect a tip for longer journeys, usually around 10%.

Tourist information

Tourist information centres (TICs) can be found in most towns. Their addresses, phone numbers and opening hours are listed in the relevant sections of this book. Opening hours vary depending on the time of year, and many of the smaller offices are closed or have limited opening hours during the winter months. All tourist offices provide information on accommodation, public transport, local attractions and restaurants, as well as selling books, local guides, maps and souvenirs. Many also have free street plans and leaflets describing local walks. They can also book accommodation for a small fee.

Museums, galleries and historic houses

Over 300 stately homes, gardens and countryside areas, are cared for by the **National Trust** ① *T0844-800 1895, www.nationaltrust.org.uk.* If you're going to be visiting several sights during your stay, then it's worth taking annual membership, which costs £53, £25 if you're aged under 26 and £70 for a family, giving free access to all National Trust properties.

A similar organization is **English Heritage** ① *T0870-333 1181, www.english-heritage.org.uk,* which manages hundreds of ancient monuments and other sights around England, including Stonehenge, and focuses on restoration and preservation. Membership includes free admission to sites, and advance information on events, and costs £47 per adult to £82 per couple, under-19s free.

Natural England ① *T0845-600 3078, www.naturalengland.org.uk,* is concerned with restoring and conserving the English countryside, and can give information on walks and events in the countryside.

Many other historic buildings are owned by local authorities, and admission is cheap, or in many cases free. Most municipal **art galleries** and **museums** are free, as well as most state-owned museums, particularly those in London and other large cities. Most fee-paying attractions give a discount or concession for senior citizens, the unemployed, full-time students and children under 16 (those under five are admitted free in most places). Proof of age or status must be shown.

Finding out more

The best way of finding out more information is to contact Visit England (aka the English Tourist Board), www.visitengland.com. Alternatively, you can contact VisitBritain, the organization responsible for tourism. Both organizations can provide a wealth of free literature and information such as maps, city guides and accommodation brochures. Travellers with special needs should also contact VisitEngland or their nearest VisitBritain office. If you want more detailed information on a particular area, contact the specific tourist boards; see in the main text for details.

Visas and immigration

Visa regulations are subject to change, so it is essential to check with your local British embassy, high commission or consulate before leaving home. Citizens of all European countries – except Albania, Bosnia Herzegovina, Kosovo, Macedonia, Moldova, Turkey, Serbia and all former Soviet republics (other than the Baltic states) – require only a passport to enter Britain and can generally stay for up to 3 months. Citizens of Australia, Canada, New Zealand, South Africa or the USA can stay for up to 6 months, providing they have a return ticket and sufficient funds to cover their stay. Citizens of most other countries require a visa from the commission or consular office in the country of application.

The UK Border Agency, www.ukba.homeoffice.gov.uk, is responsible for UK immigration matters and its website is a good place to start for anyone hoping visit, work, study or emigrate to the UK. For visa extensions also contact the UK Border Agency via the website. Citizens of Australia, Canada, New Zealand, South Africa or the USA wishing to stay longer than 6 months will need an Entry Clearance Certificate from the British High Commission in their country. For more details, contact your nearest British embassy, consulate or high commission, or the Foreign and Commonwealth Office in London.

Weights and measures

Imperial and metric systems are both in use. Distances on roads are measured in miles and yards, drinks poured in pints and gills, but generally, the metric system is used elsewhere.

Contents

Devon

Devon, England's biggest and most beautiful county is huntin', fishin', shootin' and farmin' country. So it rains, the roads may be impossibly busy in the middle of the day, and nothing much happens after midnight. Instead, visitors can enjoy the best cream tea of their lives, mile upon mile of well-tended organic farmland and the choice of two delightful coastlines.

The russet-red South Devon Coast became fashionable in the early 19th century, especially around the polite Regency resort of Sidmouth, while Exeter remains the administrative heart of the county. Slightly bewildered perhaps, the atmosphere of this ancient cathedral city can best be summed up as the living embodiment of the generation gap. On the coast to the south, the seaside resorts of Torbay have no such doubts – the English Riviera really does consider itself a cut above, whatever your age, even though the weather generally fails to deliver.

The prosperous land south of the river Dart, known as South Hams, contains the epicentre of free-thinking in the Southwest at Totnes as well as the Royal Naval College at Dartmouth and the boating middle-classes' favourite seaside rendezvous at Salcombe. The Navy crops up again in a big way at Plymouth, the biggest city in the county and one with an undeniable sense of its place in the history of the world. In its heyday it sent its prisoners north, to Dartmoor, still one of the most strange and eerie stretches of moorland in England.

The North Devon Coast is the most romantic wooded shoreline in the British Isles and birthplace of British surfing. It finally peters out in the west with the rocks and wilds of Hartland.

Exeter and the South Devon Coast

Exeter, at the mouth of the River Exe, is a city with a very visible generation gap. The regional capital of the Southwest, it has only fairly recently begun to cotton on to the various different ways in which today's 20- or 30-somethings like to divest themselves of their cash. There is an old-fashioned decency about the place, a pride in its central role in county affairs and in its civic status, which - though not without a certain charm - can sometimes make it seem a bit stodgy. There is more to life, after all, than a medieval cathedral (however beautiful) and a worthy provincial museum. Now attracting a youngish crowd that increasingly regards the city as a lively base from which to explore the various outdoor attractions of Devon and Cornwall, Exeter's teashops are just waking up to the fact that the shop next door is now just as likely to be selling skateboards and Pacific-style surfwear, than it is sensible shoes and tweed caps. At the forefront of this revolution, the Quayside development down on the river is in the process of carving out the kind of space familiar to many European cities: a stretch of water to perambulate by, a slight whiff of culture, and a selection of bars, cafés, restaurants and nightclubs for the discerning punter.

East of Exeter, the Jurassic Coast (officially known as the Dorset and East Devon Coast World Heritage Site) runs from Orcombe Point to Old Harry Rocks on the Isle of Purbeck. There's a wonderful beach walk from lovely Branscombe, just past the little fishing village of Beer, to the Regency resort of Sidmouth. Very different from Lyme, Sidmouth just about preserves the memory of more formal pleasures taken in past times, coming fully alive once a year with an international folk festival. Inland, the mini- cathedral at Ottery St Mary is also worth a look, while the market town of Honiton is one of the antique dealing centres of the Southwest. Exmouth itself, round the corner from the polite retirement homes at Budleigh Salterton, is a straightforward low-rent seaside town for family holiday fun.

Visiting Exeter and the South Devon Coast

Getting there
Exeter International Airport is 6 miles out of the city. **Stagecoach** (www.stagecoach bus.com) operates a regular bus – Service 56 – between the airport and Exeter St Davids rail station, bus station and Exmouth. Exeter is well served by rail. From London trains depart about once an hour from both Paddington (2 hours 20 minutes) and Waterloo (3 hours 20 minutes). The Waterloo trains, though a lot slower, have the advantage of depositing you at Exeter Central, right in the middle of the city, while the Paddington trains go to Exeter St Davids, a 15-minute walk, or a short taxi or bus ride (take the H) into town. Axminster is the closest mainline station to Seaton, with a regular bus service 885 to the coast. Honiton is the closest mainline station to Sidmouth, connected by bus service 52B. **National Rail Enquiries**, T08457-484950, www.nationalrail.co.uk. From London, the safe bet is to stick to the M4 and M5 motorways getting off at junction 30 (about 3 hours). The M3/A303/A30 route is more direct and more interesting, but it is by no means dual carriageway all the way, so you can find yourself stuck behind a lorry or a caravan, especially at peak holiday times. There are plenty of car parks in the city centre, where 24-hour parking costs from £6. Matford Park & Ride is located to the south of the city centre, off the A379. **National Express**, T08717-818178, www.nationalexpress.com,

operate coaches to Exeter from most parts of the country. Exmouth and Budleigh Salterton are both easily reached by bus from Exeter. **Traveline**, www.travelinesw.com. ►► *See Transport, page 31.*

Getting around
The centre of Exeter is compact enough to negotiate on **foot**. Regular buses, run by **First** in Dorset, Empress Road, Southampton, T08700-010 6022, www.firstgroup.com/ ukbus/dorset, and **Stagecoach South West**, Belgrave Rd, Exeter, T01392-427711, www.stagecoachbus.com, connect Lyme Regis with Seaton, Sidmouth, Budleigh Salterton and Exmouth. **Axe Valley Mini Travel**, 26 Harbour Rd, Seaton, T01297- 625959, run a coastal service from Seaton via Beer and Branscombe to Sidmouth.

Tourist information
Budleigh Salterton TIC ⓘ *Fore St, T01395-445275. Exmouth, Manor Gardens, Alexandra Terr, T01395-222299. Axminster TIC, The Old Courthouse, Church Street, T01297-34386.* **Exeter Visitor Information & Tickets** ⓘ *Dix's Field, Princesshay Quarter, T01392-665700, www.exeter.gov.uk. Apr-Sep Mon-Sat 0900-1700 Oct-Mar, Mon-Sat 0930-1630, bank holidays 1000-1600.* Pick up a copy of *The List*, Exeter's free listings magazine to find out what's on. **Seaton TIC and Seaton Tramway Ticket Office** ⓘ *The Underfleet, T01297-21660, www.seatontic.com.* **Sidmouth TIC** ⓘ *Ham La, T01395-516441, www.visit sidmouth.co.uk.*

Exeter → *For listings, see pages 28- 31.*

The war did little for modern Exeter and, although the cathedral quarter around the twin-towered St Peter's Cathedral offers a glimpse of how it must have been, it is mostly a place to shop today: the attractive Princesshay centre is a place to find names from Apple to Zara, while Fore Street hosts the weekly farmers' market.

Background
Historically, traces of an early settlement at this shallow, fordable bend in the river go back a couple of hundred years BC. It was not until the Romans built a legionary fortress here in AD 55, though, that the city began to take its place on the map. The Romans departed in 410, leaving a robust set of city walls which, repaired by King Alfred in the ninth century to keep out the marauding Danes, remain in parts to this day. The next set of invaders, the Normans, gave the city its greatest foreign legacy: the two towers of the cathedral, whose main body was rebuilt in medieval times. Exeter also retains some fine examples of medieval architecture, despite the attentions of Hitler's Luftwaffe which, in a bombing raid on 4 May 1942, destroyed great swathes of the old centre, most of it – regrettably – replaced by unprepossessing, uninspired examples of 1960s architecture.

Places in Exeter
A good place to begin a tour of the city is outside the **Royal Clarence Hotel** looking out onto the Cathedral Green. On your left are **Mol's Coffee Shop** – now selling maps – allegedly an old Tudor haunt of Sir Francis Drake and St Martin's Church, and an

interesting little red sandstone church dedicated in 1065; whilst ahead of you is the sedentary figure of Richard Hooker, the great Anglican theologian of the 16th century, who – on a summer's day – is surrounded by people recumbent in less formal postures on the grass. The **cathedral** itself is named after St Peter, who stands naked with a fishing net in his hands at the apex of the building, a recent, 1980s addition to the other statues of the 14th/15th century image screen. Once inside the impressive, vaulted nave, look out for the minstrels' gallery on the north side, with its 14 musical angels, and the 15th-century astronomical clock in the north transept. Wander past the gigantic oak Bishop's Throne, dated 1312, near the altar and explore the series of intimate chapels that surround the north end of the chancel. The Exeter Rondels, the tapestry cushions that line both sides of the nave, form a fascinating record in pictures and text of Exeter's history from Roman times right up to 1983, having taken 65 local ladies 4 years and 14 million stitches to complete.

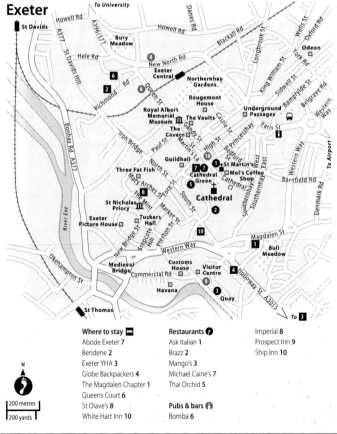

Exeter

Where to stay 🛏
Abode Exeter **7**
Bendene **2**
Exeter YHA **3**
Globe Backpackers **4**
The Magdalen Chapter **1**
Queens Court **6**
St Olave's **8**
White Hart Inn **10**

Restaurants 🍴
Ask Italian **1**
Brazz **2**
Mango's **3**
Michael Caine's **7**
Thai Orchid **5**

Pubs & bars 🍸
Bomba **6**

Imperial **8**
Prospect Inn **9**
Ship Inn **10**

N

200 metres
200 yards

Retrace your steps past the **Royal Clarence Hotel** up St Martin's Lane, a narrow alleyway leading onto the High Street. A few yards to the left is the **Guildhall** ① *T01392-665500, limited opening times, free,* quite possibly the oldest municipal building in the country. Straight ahead of you, down Queen Street, is the revamped **Royal Albert Memorial Museum** ① *T01392-265858, www.rammuseum.org.uk, Tue-Sat 1000-1700, free,* which features exhibitions on archaeology, geology, zoology, fine art, costumes and world cultures . Tucked away to the right and parallel to Queen Street is the cobbled Gandy Street, home to some quirky boutiques and cafés. Further to the right up the High Street, a left turn up Castle Street will take you to the gardens of **Rougemont House**, containing some of the original walls of William I's castle and a memorial to the last four witches to be hanged in Devon in 1685. In Romangate Passage, next to **Boots**, you have the opportunity to descend into the **Underground Passages** ① *T01392-665887, Jun-Sep Mon-Sat 1000-1700, Sun 1030-1600, Oct-May Tue-Fri 1130-1730, Sat 0930-1730, Sun 1130-1600, £5.50, child £4, family £17,* a network of 14th-century tunnels used to bring fresh water into the city.

Heading back along the High Street, continue over the brow of the hill into Fore Street down towards the Quay. Right, along a street called The Mint, is the 11th-century **St Nicholas Priory** ① *T01392-265858, Easter-Oct Mon-Sat 1400-1630, £3.50, child £1.50,* containing an exhibition about the history of the Devon and Dorset Regiment. **Tuckers Hall** ① *T01392-412348, www.tuckershall.org.uk, 1030-1300 Tue, Thu and Fri in summer, Thu and first Sat of each month at other times, free,* further down Fore Street, is the guildhall of the weavers, fullers and shearmen of Exeter, with a barrel roof and attractive panelling. Take a quick look, in front of you, at the city's **medieval bridge**, now marooned on dry land in the middle of a traffic gyratory system, before turning left and down onto the Quay. There, amongst the bars and cafés, you will find a handsome 17th-century **Customs House** ① *T01392-265213, daily 1000-1700 Apr-Oct, weekends only 1100-1600 Nov-Mar, free,* with a Visitor Centre, containing a display about the history of the Quay and an audio-visual story of Exeter. The Quay is also the place to hire a bicycle or canoe to head out into the waterways and countryside of the Exe estuary, see What to do, page 30.

Finally, the **Exeter University campus** ① *T01392-263999, weekdays 0900-1800 and Sat mornings, free,* on a site about a mile outside the centre, contains a sculpture walk – including works by Barbara Hepworth and Henry Moore – and a fine botanical garden.

South Devon Coast → *For listings, see pages 28- 31.*

East of Exeter, the Jurassic Coast (officially known as the Dorset and East Devon Coast World Heritage Site) runs from Orcombe Point to Old Harry Rocks on the Isle of Purbeck. There's a wonderful beach walk from lovely Branscombe, just past the little fishing village of Beer, to the Regency resort of Sidmouth. Very different from Lyme, Sidmouth just about preserves the memory of more formal pleasures taken in past times, coming fully alive once a year with an international folk festival. Inland, the mini- cathedral at Ottery St Mary is also worth a look, while the market town of Honiton is one of the antique dealing centres of the Southwest. Exmouth itself, round the corner from the polite retirement homes at Budleigh Salterton, is a straightforward low-rent seaside town for family holiday fun.

Walks in Devon

- **Wistman's Wood**, Dartmoor: 4 mile circle. Start: Two Bridges. Twisted dwarf oaks and mossy boulders in a mysterious wood 2 miles north of Two Bridges. OS Maps: Outdoor Leisure 28.
- **Buckland Beacon**, Dartmoor: 2 miles there and back. Start: Buckland-in-the-Moor. A short walk up to one of the moor's finest viewpoints. OS Maps: Outdoor Leisure 28.
- **Exmoor**: 4-mile circle. Start: Simonsbath. Riverside walks southeast of the village down the Barle to the hill fort at Cow Castle. OS Maps: Outdoor Leisure 9.
- **North Devon Coast**: 3 mile circle. Start: Woody Bay, 3 miles west of Lynmouth. Clifftop and woodland walks past the inspiration for the Coleridge's 'Rhyme of the Ancient Mariner'. OS Maps: Outdoor Leisure 9.
- **South Devon Coast**: 6 miles there and back. Start: Beer, 10 miles west of Lyme Regis. Along the South West Coast path to Branscombe and back. OS Maps: Explorer 116/115.

Seaton

Six miles west of Lyme Regis, past the landslip nature reserve, at the mouth of the river Axe, Seaton has a small harbour, prom and seaside amusements, and a long pebble beach backed by beach huts. It's popular with families and birdwatchers, who enjoy the nostalgic trips on the open-air double-decker trams that run from here to Colyford and Coltyon (**Seaton Tramway**, T01297-20375, www.tram.co.uk), whistling their way up the pretty floodplain and alongside the nature reserve of the Axe valley.

Beer

The coast becomes more picturesque a little further on, at the tiny little fishing village of Beer. Very twee, with the **Anchor Inn** on the seafront, ragstone walls and a few small boats, its small pebbly beach is also sheltered by limestone cliffs. On sunny days it can become almost Mediterranean. The village was once home to the most notorious smuggler in the Southwest, Jack Rattenbury, who would certainly have been familiar with the warren of **caverns** ① *T01297-680282, www.beerquarrycaves.co.uk, £6.80, child £5, family £21*, carved into the hill at its main low-key tourist attraction today, Beer's 2000-year-old stone **quarry**. The chilly quarry provided material for buildings like Exeter and Winchester Cathedrals and also a secret Catholic chapel.

Branscombe

Branscombe is another picture-postcard thatched village 2 miles west, with a wonderful wide pebbly **beach** protected by the National Trust and good walks all around. The Trust also runs the **Old Bakery tearoom** in the village, next to the **Manor Mill** and still-working **Old Forge** ① *T01297-680333, www.nationaltrust.org.uk, Old Bakery Easter-Jul, Sep-Oct Wed-Sun 1030-1700, Aug daily 1030-1700, Manor Mill Apr-Oct Sun (also Wed in Jul and Aug) 1400-1700, £1, Old Forge T01297-680481, daily 1000-1700*. The **Millennium Rose garden** just above the church is spectacular, laid out on the slopes of a combe heading down to the sea. From here a 7-mile beach walk to Sidmouth passes lost coves only accessible from the sea, and places where potatoes were once grown on the undercliff. At **Salcombe Regis**, a footpath leads a mile down to another lonely beach, from the old church with its rare cherry tree, half a mile from the sea. Just beyond Weston, the world's largest donkey sanctuary is at **Slade House Farm** ① *T01395-578222, www.thedonkeysanctuary.org.uk, daily 0900-dusk, free,* home to about 200 of the "devil's walking parody of all four-footed things" as GK Chesterton called them, their days of working the beaches done.

Sidmouth

Sidmouth, approached from the west through another deep wooded dell with fine beech trees, is a sight to behold, sitting snug between its russet-red cliffs basking in the southern sun looking out to sea. A speculative development of a certain Emmanuel Lousada at the close of the 18th century, the town became one of the most fashionable and exclusive seaside resorts on the south coast. Here, even more than the Torbay resorts round the corner, was somewhere that really did rival the Riviera. A fair bit of the architecture from those glory days survives, some of it along the Esplanade, but more especially in the *cottages ornés* that decorate the slopes up Glen Road and Bickwell Valley, beyond the Victoria and Royal Glen Hotels, where Princess Victoria stayed with her parents in 1819. Lousada overlooked his creation from Peak House, which still stands above the fine Connaught Gardens on the seafront.

The whole town has become famous for its flower displays and clings on to its dignity even in high summer, remaining fairly unspoilt with a sandy area of beach and good rockpools at low tide at the Jacob's Ladder end of the seafront. The **Sidmouth Museum** ① *Hope Cottage, Church St, T01395- 516139, www.sidvaleassociation.org.uk, Apr-Oct Mon 1300-1600,Tue-Sat 1000-1600, free,* is full of photos of the town in its heyday, a geological display on the Jurassic Coast, and staff lead free guided tours of the town on Tuesdays and Thursdays at 1100 and Wednedays at 1400. Otherwise, you can enjoy descending to **Jacob's Ladder** on the Western Beach from Connaught Gardens, strolling along the Esplanade and admiring the Georgian architecture of York Terrace behind, browsing in the shops up Fore St or climbing the steep footpath up **Salcombe Hill Cliff** east of the town.

Inland from Sidmouth

Eight miles inland from Sidmouth, through **Sidbury** with its seventh-century crypt in the church ① *Jul-Sep Thu 1400-1700,* **Honiton** is a prosperous market town, dominated by its 104-ft church tower and a large number of antique shops and auction houses. A good place to browse, the **Thelma Hubert Gallery** ① *Elmfield House, Dowell St, T01404-45006, www.thelmahulbert.com, Feb-Dec Tue-Sat 1000-1700, free,* is also worth a look, a public art space for changing exhibitions of work by local artists as well as international names thanks to its links with the Hayward Gallery in London.

Ottery St Mary, 7 miles west towards Exeter, has one of the most remarkable parish churches in the West Country, partially constructed in 1260 and remodelled on Exeter Cathedral around 1340. It too has an astronomical clock, in the south transept, believed to date from the late 14th century and an equally ancient weathervane on the tower. In the vicarage next door, Samuel Taylor Coleridge was born in 1772, 13th child of the vicar of St Mary's. A mile to the northwest, **Cadhay Manor** ① *T01404-813511, www.cadhay.org.uk, May-Sep Fri 1400-1730, spring and Aug bank holidays, guided tours £7, £3 child, gardens only £3, £1 child,* is a peaceful medieval house with Elizabethan and Georgian alterations, the interior shown on guided tours.

Exmouth and around

From Otterton Mill, a 2-mile footpath leads downriver to the Otter's mouth at **Budleigh Salterton**. No prom here to speak of, but instead a curving pebbly beach under the russet-red cliffs, with their pebbled seams, and an atmosphere that provides a foretaste of genteel South Hams round the corner. A little thatched house contains the **Fairlynch Museum** ⓘ *27 Fore St, T01395-442666, Easter-Oct daily 1400-1630, free*, with displays on costume, social history and geology.

Next door, **Exmouth's** broad sweep of sandy beach fronts a faintly neglected esplanade, nonetheless popular for family-holiday fun, with fish and chips aplenty and donkey rides on the beach in summer. Boat trips run across the mouth of the river Exe to **Powderham Castle** and the even larger beach at **Dawlish Warren**.

Just outside Exmouth off the Exeter road is the world-famous folly house, **A La Ronde** ⓘ *Summer La, Exmouth, T01395-265514, www.national-trust.org.uk, Feb-Oct daily 1100-1700, £7.50, under-16s £3.80, family £18.80,* built with 16 sides to the designs of the Parminter spinsters, Jane and Mary, apparently inspired by the church of San Vitale in Ravenna. Completed in 1798, it still displays the fruits of their 18th-century Grand Tour of Europe and their curious taste in interior design: a shell-decorated gallery (only viewable via CCTV), and a feather frieze. Only once owned by a man, the house can be compared with the Parminters' other pet project, up the road, called 'Point of View', a chapel and almshouses purpose-built for single women only.

Exeter and South Devon Coast listings

For hotel and restaurant price codes and other relevant information, see pages 9-13.

🛏 Where to stay

Exeter *p22, map p23*

££££-£££ Abode Exeter (formerly the Royal Clarence Hotel), Cathedral Yard, T01392-319955, www.abodehotels.co.uk. The first English inn to use the French term 'hotel', its regal site at the very heart of the city injects a sense of history and occasion.

£££ The Magdalen Chapter, Magdalen St, T01392-281000, www.themagdalen chapter.com. Exeter's biggest surprise. A funky, Gaudi-inspired designer fantasy and Exeter landmark, in what used to be the West of England Eye Infirmary. There's a stylish restaurant and a spa with a pool, gym and treatment rooms.

£££ Queens Court Hotel, 6/8 Bystock Terr, T01392-272709, www.queens court-hotel.co.uk. Family-run hotel, in central location, with an award-winning restaurant.

£££-££ St Olave's, Mary Arches St, T01392-217736, www.olaves.co.uk. Intimate, characterful hotel in an elegant Georgian merchant's house with its own walled garden.

££ Bendene Hotel, 15-16 Richmond Rd, T01392-213526, www.bendene.co.uk. A 5-min walk, over the iron bridge, to the cathedral. Good value, with outdoor pool. Free Wi-Fi and parking.

££ White Hart Inn, 66 South St, T01392-279897, www.whitehartpubexeter.co.uk. The genuine article. A real 14th-century coaching inn, all beams, flagged floors and dark panelled rooms.

££-£ Exeter YHA, Mount Wear House, 47 Countess Wear Rd, Countess Wear, T01392-371 9516, www.yha.org.uk. Exeter's youth hostel is 4 miles out of the city on the way to the pretty estuary town of Topsham.

£ Globe Backpackers, 71 Holloway St, T01392-215521, www.exeterback packers.co.uk. Centrally located hostel, with communal TV lounge, dining area and kitchen.

South Devon Coast *p24*

££££ Combe House Hotel, Gittisham, near Honiton, T01404-540400, www.combehousedevon.com. An Elizabethan manor house hotel with an exceptional restaurant and lovely quiet grounds.

££££ Hotel Riviera, The Esplanade, Sidmouth, T01395-515201, www.hotelriviera.co.uk. The grandest of the town's Regency hotels.

£££ Royal York and Faulkner Hotel, Sidmouth, T0800-220714, www.royalyorkhotel.co.uk. Considerably less expensive than the **Hotel Riviera**, but also in a good position on the Esplanade.

£££-££ Masons Arms, Main St, Branscombe, T01297-680300, www.masonsarms.co.uk. A large pub and hotel with reasonable food in the middle of the village, thatched roof and even thatched umbrellas outside.

££ Bay View Guest House, Beer, T01297-20489, www.bayviewbeer.com. Right on the seafront and South West Coast Path with lovely views. Breakfast and parking included.

££ Glendevon Hotel, Cotmaton Rd, Sidmouth, T01395-514028, www.glendevonsidmouth.co.uk. A good option, tucked up Glen Rd.

££ Lower Pinn Farm B&B, Peak Hill, Sidmouth, T01395-513733, www.lower pinnfarm.co.uk. In an excellent position on the coast road beyond Peak Hill to the west. Friendly and comfortable farmhouse accommodation.

££ Mariner's B&B, The Esplanade, Seaton, T01297-20560, www.marinershotel

seaton.co.uk. Good seafront option with views across Lyme Bay towards Beer Head.
££-£ Beer YHA, Bovey Combe, Beer, T01297- 20296. At the top of the town, above the Pecorama gardens, 40 beds in an airy country house in an Arts and Crafts style.

🍴 Restaurants

Exeter *p22, map p23*
£££ Michael Caine's, Abode Exeter, see Where to stay, T01392-223638. Part of the growing empire of the eponymous award-winning chef and the poshest venue in town.
££ Ask Italian, 5 Cathedral Cl, T01392-427127, www.askitalian.co.uk. Its setting within the elegant, panelled rooms of an ancient, ecclesiastical building right next door to the cathedral gives this dependable Italian restaurant a real touch of class.
££ Brazz, 10-12 Palace Gate, T01392-252525. A tropical fish tank dominates the modern interior of this stylish brasserie-bar-café. Cheaper express menu at lunchtime.
££ Thai Orchid, The Three Gables, Cathedral Yard, T01392-214215, www.thai orchidrestaurant.co.uk. Welcoming Thai eatery with a good reputation, looking onto the cathedral. Choose from set menus or à la carte main dishes. Also cheaper set lunch menu and takeaway.
£ Mango's, King's Wharf, The Quay, T01392- 438538. Colourful, friendly café serving sandwiches, salads, tortilla wraps, cakes, teas and breakfasts at reasonable prices.

South Devon Coast *p24*
££ Fountain Head, Street, just up from Branscombe, T01297-680359, www.fountainheadinn.com. Seafood and own-brew beers in a cosy and ramshackle little place, also with benches on logs outside.
££ The Galley, 41 Fore St, Topsham, T01392-876078, www.galleyrestaurant.co.uk.

Very good fish restaurant looking out to sea downriver, although it's quite expensive.
£ The Dolphin, Beer, T01297-24506, www.dolphinhotelbeer.co.uk. Does huge portions of fish and chips and has a small garden.
£ Kingfisher, Dolphin St, Colyton, T01297-552476, www.kingfisherinn.co.uk. A friendly local in a once-prosperous wool town, a good stop on the Seaton Tramway.

🍺 Pubs, bars and clubs

Exeter *p22, map p23*
Bar Bomba, 44 Queen St, T01392-412233. Bar Bomba has brought cocktails and lounge living to Queen St – 60 different ones – in this Latin American Cuban Caribbean subterranean space, with a restaurant on ground level.
Double Locks, Canal Banks, T01392-256947, www.doublelocks.com. Hire a canoe or a cycle and head down to this very popular riverside pub, serving good food, a mile and a half away from the Quayside.
The Imperial, New North Rd, T01392-434050. Grand, old mansion near the university. Very cheap drinks at the Monday Club and an orangery designed by Isambard Kingdom Brunel.
The Prospect Inn, The Quayside, T01392-273152. Lots of different levels, nooks, crannies and fireplaces – and a fairly bogus nautical theme. The best place for a pint down on the Quayside.
The Ship Inn, St Martin's La, T01392-272040. Reputedly a watering hole of Francis Drake and Walter Raleigh, this busy, low-ceilinged pub just off Cathedral Yard still retains a certain olde-worlde charm.

Clubs and live music

The club scene is getting steadily more sophisticated, though the contrast between streetlife on Fri and Sat nights (adolescent, alcoholic mayhem) and the rest of the week (quite quiet, really) is still marked.

The Cavern, 83 Queen St, T01392-495370, exetercavern.com. At the forefront of live music in Exeter, with a particular emphasis on punk, indie and hard rock. Also has drum'n'bass DJs.

Havana, The Quayside, T01392-459888. Live music, comedy and salsa in this club.

Timepiece, Little Castle St, T01392-493096, www.timepiecenightclub.co.uk. Offers a variety of nights, from salsa, merengue and samba, to drum n bass and dubstep.

The Vaults, 8 Gandy St, T01392-203939, www.vaultsexeter.co.uk. Predominantly gay clientele in this underground bar with regular cabaret, karaoke and theme nights.

South Devon Coast *p24*
£ The Bridge Inn, Bridge Hill, Topsham, south of Exeter, T01392-873862, www.cheffers.co.uk. Excellent sandwiches, tables by the creek and rambling old rooms inside, very friendly landlord and superb real ales.

😊 Entertainment

Exeter *p22, map p23*
Cinema
The Exeter Picture House, Bartholomew St, off Fore St, T0871-902 5730. Has a lively bar.

The Odeon, Sidwell St, at the north end of the High St, 0871-224 4007.

Theatres and other arts venues
The city's premier drama venue, the **Northcott Theatre**, is on the university campus, T01392-493493, www.exeternorthcott.co.uk, though it stages an annual outdoor show in the Rougemont Gardens. There's also **The Phoenix** art centre, Bradninch Pl, just off Gandy St, T01392-667080, www.exeterphoenix.org.uk.

🎪 Festivals

Exeter *p22, map p23*
Jun Ignite: Exeter's Festival of Theatre 9-day celebration in early Jun, www.igniteexeter.org.uk.

South Devon Coast *p24*
Aug Sidmouth Folk Week, tickets T01395-577952, www.sidmouthfolkweek.co.uk. Starting on the Friday before the first Mon of every Aug for a week, Sidmouth hosts this internationally famous event drawing in aficionados from all over the world, with the main events selling out.

🏔 What to do

Exeter *p22, map p23*
Boat trips
Stuart Line Cruises, T01395-222144, www.stuartlinecruises.co.uk. Operate boat trips on the River Exe and along the Jurassic Coast.

Tours
The Red Coats, T01392-265203, www.exeter.gov.uk/guidedtours. These are a collection of local history enthusiasts, who share their expertise in a wide variety of daily tours conducted throughout the year, including, for instance, a catacomb experience concentrating on death and burial in the city.

Watersports
Haven Banks Outdoor Education Centre, T01392-434668, www.haven-banks.co.uk for canoeing in the Exe Estuary and other watersports.

⊖ Transport

Exeter *p22, map p23*

Air
Exeter International Airport runs flights to **Dublin**, **Belfast**, **Edinburgh**, **Glasgow**, **Manchester**, **Newcastle**, **Guernsey**, **Jersey**, **Scilly Isles**, and a wide variety of international destinations.

Bicycle
Saddles and Paddles, on the Quayside, T01392-424241, www.sadpad.com. For hiring out bikes.

Bus
Stagecoach, run the 56 service hourly to Exeter Airport (30 mins). **National Express**, T08717-818178, run directly 4 times daily to **Plymouth** (1hr 5 mins), 4 times to **Bristol** (1 hr 50 mins), 8 times to **London Paddington** (4 hrs 30 mins) and directly to **Bournemouth** (3 hrs 35 mins) at 1135. Contact **Traveline**, T0871-200 2233, www.traveline.org.uk, for local bus information.

Car
Avis, Exeter International Airport, T08445-446015; **Thrifty**, 12 Marsh Barton Rd, T01392-207207.

Taxi
A1 Cars, 54 Queen St, T01392-218888; **Castle Cars**, 81 Victoria St, T01392-436363.

Train
Virgin Trains, T08719-774222, run the services twice hourly direct to **Plymouth** (1 hr 5 mins) and regularly direct to **Bristol Temple Meads** (1 hr 15 mins). **First Great Western**, T08457-000125, run the hourly direct service to **London Paddington** (2 hrs 20 mins to 3 hrs). There is no direct service to Bournemouth or Exeter Airport. Exeter St Davids also connects with trains north to **Birmingham**, south into **Cornwall** and operates the Dawlish Donkey steam service to **Paignton** in the summer.

ⓘ Directory

Exeter *p22, map p23*
Hospitals Royal Devon and Exeter Hospital, Gladstone Rd, T01392-411611.

Torbay and South Hams

The coast between Dawlish and Brixham is the place for an urban coastal holiday, complete with Walls ice cream, fish and chips and crazy golf. Sheltered from the prevailing southwesterlies, there are water parks, go-karts and buckets and spades, along with the pink sand the locals claim is the best ever for sandcastles.

However, alongside this, a new spirit is abroad, seen in the refurbished harbour in Torquay. As retro becomes chic, it looks like the in-crowd are coming, enjoying the calm waters, scudding yacht sails and regular visits of tall ships.

Visiting Torbay and South Hams

Getting there
The main express line from London Paddington to Plymouth via Exeter usually calls at Newton Abbot. Otherwise, regular services from Exeter St Davids run to Exeter St Thomas, Dawlish, Teignmouth, Newton Abbot, Torre, Torquay, Paignton and Totnes. **National Rail Enquiries**, T08457-484950,www.nationalrail.co.uk.

From the M5 at Exeter take the A380 for Torquay, Paignton and Brixham, the A379 for Dawlish.

Stagecoach South West, T01392-427711, www.stagecoachbus.com run the No 85 bus from Exeter every 30 minutes to Dawlish Warren, Teignmouth, Shaldon and Torquay. Bus No 12 links Torquay with Paignton and Brixham. There are regular bus services from Newton Abbot to Totnes. **Tally Ho!**, T01548-853081, www.tallyhocoaches.co.uk, run service No 164 between Totnes and Kingsbridge and No 606 between Kingsbridge and Salcombe.

Getting around
Regular local **bus** services make it easy to hop around Torbay, although these too can get caught up in holiday traffic. A bicycle would be the best bet, although the rolling roads can be punishing on Shanks's pony. The **Dawlish Donkey** ① *T0871-8714119*, is a hop-on, hop-off steam train that runs from Exeter to Paignton in Aug during the week, departing Exeter at 0935 and 1440, arriving at Paignton (calling at Dawlish Warren, Dawlish and Torquay) at 1050 and 1545.

Unfortunately a car is the most efficient way of exploring South Hams, and if there weren't as many of those, then a bike would be much more fun. The tiny lanes between Dartmouth, Kingsbridge and Salcombe are often quite dangerous for cyclists in summer.

Tourist information
Brixham TIC ① *Hob Nobb's Gift Shop, The Quay, T0844-474 2233*. **Dawlish TIC** ① *The Lawn, T01626-215665*. **English Riviera Visitor Information Centre, Vaughan Parade, Torquay,** ① *T0844-474 2233, www.theenglishriviera.co.uk*. **Paignton TIC** ① *The Esplanade, T01803-55383*. **Teignmouth TIC** ① *The Den, T01626-215666, www.visitsouth devon.co.uk*. **Totnes TIC** ① *The Town Mill, Coronation Rd, T01803-863168*. Open all year.

Around Torbay → *For listings, see page 36.*

The river Exe finally finds the sea at Dawlish Warren sands, opposite Exmouth and about 10 miles south of Exeter. The sheltered east-facing coastline that then runs south from here has long been dubbed the 'English Riviera'. Although finding any similarities to the Cote d'Azur can test the imagination, its situation, temperate climate and cabbage palms probably come as close as England gets. Torquay, the capital of the region, is certainly stacked up on Hope's Nose, a headland faintly reminiscent of St Tropez, if you like, overlooking the sweep of Tor Bay to the south. It even boasts a tiny corniche road twisting down to Babbacombe Bay in the north. Down beside the seaside, Paignton is its more family-orientated neighbour, with the busiest sandy beaches, while the fishing town of Brixham nestles further south on Berry Head. This distinctive threesome adds up to the south Devon coast at its most marketed, most visited and often most congested.

A ferry ride away across the mouth of the Exe from Exmouth, or a couple of miles south of Exeter by road, **Powderham Castle** ① *T01626-890243, www.powderham.co.uk, Apr-Oct Sun-Fri, Sun 1100-1630 (or 1730 during summer holidays), £10.50, under-16s £8.50, concessions £5.95, family £15.85,* is the rambling ancestral home of the Earl of Devon. In the late 18th century, long before the scandal surrounding Oscar Wilde, it was here that William Beckford met the aesthetic 13-year-old William Courtenay, with disastrous effects on both their social lives. William Courtenay's refined taste is preserved in the domed music room of the castle, which today is also a full-on visitor attraction, complete with pet's corner, miniature railway, and medieval jousting. There are beautiful views of the Exe from the Belvedere in the woods.

Another very different stately home can be found 8 miles southwest at **Ugbrooke** ① *Ugbrooke House, T01626-852179, www.ugbrooke.co.uk, mid-July to early Sep Tue, Wed, Thu, Sun, bank holidays 1230-1730, £8.80, under-16s £6.* The seat of the powerful Catholic family of Cliffords, it looks like a little toy fort, remodelled by Robert Adam in the 18th century, with a sumptuous chapel attached. The homely interior contains some remarkable portraits (including one of the rebellious Duke of Monmouth), tapestries and furniture and the lakeside grounds were laid out by – you guessed it – Capability Brown, now a little spoiled by the dual carriageways close by.

On the coast 6 miles directly east, Dawlish is a dignified retirement resort, famous for the steam train the **Dawlish Donkey** that puffs along the prom in the summer. Passengers are likely to be on their way to **Teignmouth** (pronounced Tinmouth), which Keats found very much to his liking in 1818. Today it's still quite a charming seaside town, with a pier, working harbour and the cliffside tranquility of Holcombe next door.

Torquay

Torquay is the epitome of suburbia-on-sea, immortally lampooned by John Cleese's bitter, bigoted, and frustrated hotelier in one of TV's best sitcoms *Fawlty Towers*, but still providing holidays to remember for thousands each year. Cleese no doubt drew inspiration from the town's most famous resident, Agatha Christie, who died in 1976 and lived at Ashfield House. Before her time, the great Irish playwright Sean O'Casey settled on these mild shores and even before that, William of Orange landed here in 1688 to begin the bloodless Glorious Revolution. Today the resort boasts lots of language schools, and all the usual seaside amusements, with that added frisson of class. On a warm summer evening, the twinkling lights and cafés around the harbour are just about Riviera enough. Apart from the exceptionally clean beaches, the town's other attractions include **Torre Abbey** ① *T01803-293593, www.torreabbey.co.uk, Apr-Oct daily 0930-1800 (last admission 1730), Nov-Mar Mon-Fri by appointment, £5.85, under-17s £2.50, family £13*, with its 20 historic rooms, stunning paintings and Victorian tearooms and monastic remains, small Agatha Christie room with some of her personal belongings including her typewriter, and nightgown. Not too far from here is **Kent's Cavern** ① *T01803-215136, www.kents-cavern.co.uk, Nov-Mar 1000-1630, Apr-Jun 0930-1730, Jul-Aug from 0930, Sep-Oct 0930-1700, £8.95, under-16s £8.25*, a cliff railway leads down to Babbacombe beach, open by guided tour, with geological and archaelogical explanations, in candlelight and every other type of light, taking about 45 minutes at a constant 11 degrees centigrade. Real Agatha Christie fans won't want to miss the **Torquay Museum** ① *T01803-293975, www.torquaymuseum.org, Mon-Sat 1000-1700 Apr-Oct also Sun 1330-1700, £5.15, £3.25 child*, with much more information (although less genuine artefacts than at Torre Abbey), in the Agatha Christie gallery, as well as a few BBC costumes, and from Kent's Cavern the oldest remains (31,000 years old to be precise) of modern humans in Britain. There's also an entertaining Devon farmhouse gallery.

Paignton and Brixham

Just down the road from Torquay, Paignton is the jolly one, with candy floss, toffee apples and crazy golf, and also very clean beaches. Brixham, beyond the caravan parks at Goodrington, is still a working fishing port, though a very polite one, with seafood restaurants galore and a busy yachting marina. This is where Napoleon was expected to arrive after his defeat at Waterloo, off Berry Head. Four miles to the south, **Coleton Fishacre** ① *T01803-842382, mid-Feb-Oct Sat-Thu 1030-1700, Nov-Dec Sat-Mon 1100-1600, £9, under-16s £5, family £23.60*, was designed in 1925 for the D'Oyly Cartes, the impressarios responsible for Gilbert and Sullivan. The house is a good example of the Arts and Crafts style, but is most famous for its luxuriant 25-acre exotic gardens thriving in their mild south-facing situation. They include a formal pool garden, and wild flower walks winding down to the sea. Delicate plants flourish in the microclimate here.

South Hams → *For listings, see page 36.*

West and south of Torbay, South Hams has become one of the most expensive and desirable places to live in Devon. Totnes is the capital, centre for all thinkers- with-a-difference, at the head of the wonderfully winding Dart estuary, but it's the rhomboid of pretty farmland between Dartmouth, Start Point, Salcombe and Ivybridge that has given the area its reputation for haute-cuisine and fine living. Dartmouth, across the foot ferry from Kingswear, is a naval yachting port of impeccable pedigree with a laid-back atmosphere. Salcombe is the tidiest and most picturesque of all south Devon holiday resorts. Marginally less well-known and frequented coastal treats include Bantham and Bigbury-on-Sea.

Totnes and around

Totnes, 5 miles west of Paignton, is the centre of New Age and alternative thinking in the Southwest. 'Strange Listings' of events and courses can be picked up at the museum on the High Street. A pretty town, overlooked by its redbrick church and old castle sitting on the top of the hill, its steep High Street has a formidable history. Next to a shop called **Forever England** (and next door too to the **House of Gifts**) is the **Brutus Stone**, commemorating the landing of King Brute, descendant of Aeneas, here in 1170BC according to Geoffrey of Monmouth. A right turn just beyond leads onto the Ramparts Walk, and good views round the Castle. The **Riverside Café** near the ferry port on Steamer Quay is always busy during the summer with people enjoying the river trip down to Dartmouth, and riverside walks opposite the famous Baltic Boatyards run downriver into open countryside. On the other side of the river, a little ferry leaves from the **Steampacket Inn**, taking you up to the steam railway, one of the most popular in England: **the South Devon Railway** ① *T0843-357 1420, www.southdevonrailway.co.uk, mid-Mar to Oct*, from Totnes to Buckfastleigh, on the edge of Dartmoor, calling at Staverton on its way along the banks of the Dart.

A mile from Staverton, **Dartington Hall** has beautiful terraced gardens dotted with sculpture, and has been a centre for the arts since 1925 when it was bought by the Elmhirsts. They also set up the scandal-rocked liberal public school where people like Bertrand Russell, Barbara Hepworth, Ben Nicholson, Jacob Epstein and the Freuds sent their kids. **High Cross House**, an inspiring piece of Bauhaus architecture, designed in 1936 by William Lescaze, now mounts exhibitions from the Elmhirst's art collection.

Dartmouth

Nine miles by riverboat, 16 by road from Totnes, Dartmouth is a photogenic yachting centre, with quaint eateries and B&Bs in abundance, and it's also the home of the prestigious **Royal Naval College**. Designed by Aston Webb, also responsible for Admiralty Arch on Trafalgar Square and the front of Buckingham Palace, the College looks down on the little harbour from a commanding position on the hill above. The **Butterwalk** is a Caroline half-timbered building that now houses the local history museum. Higher Street is also very picturesque, leading up to Ridge Hill and **Newcomen Lodge**, where the town's most famous son, Thomas Newcomen, developed an atmospheric steam engine in 1712.

Salcombe and around

Salcombe, 17 miles south of Totnes on the A381, is a very desirable and well-established little resort, on a picturesque estuary, with cafés overlooking the water, and even a Park and Ride. Three miles west inland, **Buckland** is a sweet little thatched village tucked away down narrow lanes, near Bantham on the sea. From here an estuary walk skirts the Avon for 9 miles, a way of crossing the river when the ferry is out of action (mid-April to October). **Bantham** itself is a string of whitewashed and dark green thatched cottages leading up the main street, to the estimable **Sloop Inn**.

West to Plymouth

On the main A379 to Plymouth, **Modbury** is a typically charming South Hams town, in a steep little valley near **Flete House**. This grand Victorian oak-panelled country house bears comparison to Castle Drogo on Dartmoor for its early-20th-century take on medievalism. At **Bigbury-on-Sea**, a sandy beach looks out towards the **Burgh Island Hotel**. Designed in 1929 in pure art deco style, facing the mainland, it was visited in its time by Noel Coward and Agatha Christie, and was also the location for John Boorman's first film *Catch Us If You Can* as well as a BBC adaptation of Christie's *Evil Under the Sun* (see Where to stay below)

Torbay and South Hams listings

For hotel and restaurant price codes and other relevant information, see pages 9-13.

☺ Where to stay

Torbay *p32*

££££ Cary Arms, Babbacombe Beach, T01803-327110, www.caryarms.co.uk. Describing itself as 'The Inn on the Beach', this chic hotel aims to combine the best of a British pub with the style and comfort of a boutique hotel. Lots of good food and accommodation (all sea-facing), including sumptuous fishermen's cottages with terraces. There's a wood-fired pizza oven and a barbecue in summer to cook local sausages. The sea and the beach are right in front and children get their own fishing net and bucket and spade for days by the rock pools.

£££ Langstone Cliff Hotel, Dawlish, T01626-868000, www.langstone-hotel.co.uk. The family who have run this waterfront hotel since 1946 are hands on in welcoming visitors and carrying out improvements. In 20 acres there are tennis courts, indoor and outdoor pools, relaxation treatments, dinner dances and cabaret weekends. A direct path leads to Warren Beach, 500 m from the hotel.

£££ The Imperial Hotel, Torquay, T01803-294301, www.pumahotels.co.uk. Top of the range in Torquay and worth the expense for the superior ambience.

£££ Nonsuch House, Church Hill, Kingswear, T01803-752829, www.hoteldartmouth.co.uk. Overlooks the mouth of the Dart, with balconies and en suite bathrooms.

££ Belmont 66 Belgrave Rd, Torquay, T01803-295028, www.thebelmont torquay.co.uk. Good value. 3-night minimum stay in high season.

££ Mulberry House, 1 Scarborough Rd, Torquay, T01803-213639, www.mulberry guesthousetorquay.co.uk. B&B rooms in a Victorian house near the centre.

South Hams *p34*

££££ Burgh Island Hotel, Bigbury-on-Sea, T01548-810514, www.burghisland.com. Restored in the 1980s by fashionistas, it's now a somewhat expensive trip down memory lane with room rates starting at over £300 per night including breakfast and dinner (1930s black tie requested). It's worth stopping for a cocktail in the bar.

££ The Dolphin Inn, Kingston, near Bigbury, T01548-810314, www.dolphin-inn.co.uk. Has 3 small rooms opposite a flowery pub in a pretty village.

££ The Sloop Inn, Bantham, T01548-560489, www.thesloop.co.uk. Does excellent bar meals and also has rooms that need to be booked well in advance during high season.

££-£ YHA Salcombe, Sharpitor, Salcombe, T0845-371 9341. On the National Trust Overbecks property with lovely gardens and coastal views, 51 beds, popular with families and always very busy in summer.

❼ Restaurants

Torbay *p32*

££ Nobody Inn, Doddiscombsleigh, T01647-252394. A popular pub in the middle of nowhere with famous food and wines.

South Hams *p34*

£££ Oyster Shack, Millburn Orchard Farm, Stake Hill, near Bigbury-on-Sea, T01548-810876, www.oystershack.co.uk. Great views towards Burgh Island and very good seafood.

££ Church House, Rattery, South Brent, T01364-642220, www.thechurchhouse inn.co.uk. Claims to be the oldest pub in the country, apparently connected to the church by a tunnel. Also has real ales.

££ Church House Inn, Harberton, near Totnes, T01803-863707, www.churchhouse harberton.co.uk. Another very ancient old pub, similarly named, with lots of oak-panelling. They serving up fresh and locally sourced food.

££ The Galley, 5 Fore St, Salcombe, T01548-842828, www.thegalleyrestaurant.co.uk. Very fresh local fish in a seafront café with spectacular estuary views.

££ Maltsters Arms, Tuckenhay, near Totnes, T01803-732350, www.tuckenhay.com. A waterside pub on a tributary of the River Dart, with Brixham fish on the menu.

££ Mill Brook, Southpool, near Kingsbridge, T01548-531581, www.millbrookinnsouth pool.co.uk. Award-winning village pub right on the waterside with excellent food.

£ The George Inn, Main St, Blackawton, T01803-712342, www.blackawton.com. A friendly village pub with exceptionally good beer.

⚠ What to do

Torbay *p32*
Boat trips
Exe 2 Sea, T01626-774770, exe2sea.co.uk. Jun-Sep. Boat trips from Dawlish seafront under the railway viaduct: half-hour trips around the bay, mackerel fishing trips lasting 1½ hrs, and 2- to 3-hr wildlife and coastal cruises. All trips are subject to weather and tides.

Greenway Ferries, T0845-489 0418, greenwayferry.co.uk. Ferries, fishing trips, geopark cruises and seafaris, operating from Torquay and Brixham, plus Dartmouth, Dittisham and Greenway.

Cycling
Forest Cycle Hire, Haldon Forest Park, T01392-833768, www.forestcyclehire.co.uk. Daily 0900-1700. Half day £12 adult, £9 child.Near the forest hub and ranger's office. A range of frame sizes for children and adults, plus tag-a-longs, child seats and buggies.

High wires
Go Ape, Haldon Forest Park, Bullers Hill, Kennford, T0845-643 9215, goape.co.uk. Mar-Oct daily in school holidays, Wed-Mon in term time; Nov Sat and Sun only. Climb and wobble between trees, safely harnessed on a high-wire forest adventure. You can stay up there for 3 hrs and enjoy a Tarzan swing into a giant rope net, zip wires through trees, crawling through tunnels and tackling high-wire rope bridges.

Horse riding
Haldon Riding Stables, Home Farm, Dunchideock, near Kennford, T01392-832645. Right below the Haldon Belvedere, 1- to 2-hr hacks through Haldon Forest Park and country lanes for both beginners and experienced riders. Lessons are also available, with an outdoor sand school.

Plymouth and Dartmoor

Heavily bombed during the war, you could argue that subsequent planning did Plymouth even fewer favours, but the fabulous location overlooking the deep bay called the Sound makes up for it, and recent investment is making it even better.

To the northeast of Plymouth is the wild expanse of Dartmoor. You could say that only mad dogs and Englishmen go out in Dartmoor weather. Though very beautiful and, occasionally sunny, it sees fog and rain even in the height of summer. However, there are things to do here year round, and the stark surroundings bring warmth – it's the kind of place where people still greet strangers as they walk or cycle past.

Visiting Plymouth and Dartmoor

Getting there
Regular direct **trains** from London Paddington take 3-3½ hours. There are also direct services to South Wales, the Midlands, the North and Scotland. Plymouth train station is about half a mile north of the city centre, at the top of Armada Way, a mile from the Hoe and Barbican. Plymouth, Exeter and Newton Abbot are the closest mainline rail stations to Dartmoor. **National Rail Enquiries**, T08457-484950, www.nationalrail.co.uk.

Plymouth is about 3½ hours-4 hours (240 miles) from London down the M5 to Exeter and then the A38. Leave London west on the M4 and continue for around 110 miles, join the M5 at junction 20 and take that southwest for around 80 miles, join the A38 after Exeter continue south for around 37 miles. Head into town on the A374. This route is usually at least 30 minutes quicker than the M3/A303 route which saves you around 15 miles in distance.

National Express, T08717-818178, www.nationalexpress.com, run a coach service taking about 4½ hours. See also **Traveline**, www.travelinesw.com. ▶▶ *See Transport, page 46.*

Getting around
The Hoe and city centre are fairly compact and can be explored on foot. Local **buses** are run by **Plymouth Citybus**, T0845-077 2223, www.plymouthbus.co.uk, and **First**, T0845-600 1420, www.firstgroup.com/ukbus/devon_cornwall. No 25 bus service runs a circular route from Plymouth railway station, along Royal Parade, through The Barbican, over The Hoe and past Plymouth Pavilions. There are many 'Pay and Display' car parks in the city centre but, owing to limited parking available in the Barbican area, it's a good idea to leave your vehicle in the multi-storey car park at Coxside and walk across the lock gates. Park & Ride facilities are available at Coypool (with buses to Drake Circus Shopping Mall) and at Milehouse and George (buses to Mayflower Street).

For walkers, a surprising amount of Dartmoor is accessible by bus. **Traveline**, www.travelinesw.com, or Devon County Council, publish annually an excellent *Discovery Guide to Dartmoor by Bus and Train*, available from most National Park and Tourist Information Centres. See also **Journey Devon**, www.journeydevon.info.

Tourist information

Plymouth TIC ① *Island House, The Barbican, T01752-306330, www.visitplymouth.co.uk. Apr-Oct Mon-Sat 0900-1700, Sun1000-1600, Nov-Mar Mon-Fri 0900-1700, Sat 1000-1600.* The main Dartmoor National Park headquarters is at **High Moorland Visitor Centre** ① *Princetown, Yelverton, T01822-890414, www.dartmoor- npa.gov.uk. Apr-Oct daily 1000-1700, Nov-Mar 1000-1600.* Other information centres can be found at the following: **Ashburton** ① *T01364-653426, Easter-end Oct 1000-1700,* **Moretonhampstead** ① *T01647-440043, Easter-end Oct 1000-1700,* **Postbridge** ① *T01822-880272, Easter-end Oct 1000-1700,* and **Haytor** ① *T01364-661520, Easter-end Oct 1000-1700.* A good range of leaflets on walks in the entire surrounding area is available at these offices and the following TICs. **Ivybridge** ① *Leonards Rd, Ivybridge, T01752-897035.* **Okehampton TIC** ① *Museum Courtyard 3, West St, T01837-53020.* **Tavistock TIC** ① *Town Hall, Bedford Sq, T01822-612938.* All are open all year round but have reduced opening times in winter.

There are also **Community Information Points** in smaller towns around the moor, such as **Buckfastleigh** ① *The Valiant Soldier, 80 Fore St, T01364-644522. Easter-Oct.* **Dartmoor Military Firing Range** ① *T0800-4584868, www.gov.uk/government/publications/dartmoor-firing-programme,* for firing times. **Forestry Commission** ① *Bullers Hill, Kennford, Exeter, T01392-834242, www.forestry.gov.uk/southwest.*

Plymouth → *For listings, see pages 45-47.*

Devon's biggest city, in a strategic setting overlooking Plymouth Sound, is even more dramatically bound up with the navy, the sea and seafaring than Portsmouth, its great naval rival on England's south coast. Epic arrivals and departures from the Sound characterize its long history, and like mercantile Liverpool, it was the launchpad of the British Empire. It too was heavily bombed during the Second World War but its subsequent redevelopment has been marginally happier than in other places. The city centre is divided by a long wide strip of lawn running south up to the Hoe which, with its superb views and memorable sense of place, is top of most visitors' list of places to visit. A 10-minute walk to the east, beneath the massive Royal Citadel, the Barbican is the oldest part of the city and site of most of its tourist attractions, including the Mayflower steps and the excellent National Marine Aquarium on Coxside.

Background

Originally a small village called Sutton, Plymouth grew up around Sutton harbour, which the Barbican's old buildings overlook to this day. The first record of a ship weighing anchor here was in 1211, almost a century before Edward I's fleet set off for France to begin the 100 Years' War. Henry VI granted the town of Plymouth a charter in 1440 and the Barbican was built in 1572. Five years later Sir Francis Drake set off in the *Golden Hind,* circling the globe before his return in 1579. Nine years on he was vice admiral of the fleet that took on the Spanish Armada, famously only after he had finished his game of bowls. In 1620 the 120 so-called Pilgrim Fathers headed west in the *Mayflower* and established the Massachusetts Bay Colony. Some of them overnighted before in Island House, 9 The Barbican, now the TIC, still recognizably a Jacobean house. Plymouth held out for Parliament during the Civil War that followed, surviving a three-year siege by the

Royalists, resulting in the construction of the intimidating Royal Citadel on the Hoe by Charles II when he was restored to the throne. In 1768, James Cook set sail to find Australia in the *Endeavour* from here and less than a century later Plymouth was to become a major embarkation point for emigrations and deportations. Between the wars, Sutton Harbour became a major fishery and in 1921 Ernest Shackleton departed on his final voyage to the Antarctic from here. More recently, in the 1980s, the Falklands Task Force followed in his wake.

Places in Plymouth

The Hoe, a stirring place to contemplate the death of Empire, is where Drake insisted on finishing his game of bowls as the Armada sailed up the channel. His statue stands here still, hand jauntily on hip, surrounded by a host of other naval greats and less-than greats, an obelisk commemorating the death of Queen Victoria's grandson at Pretoria stands out,

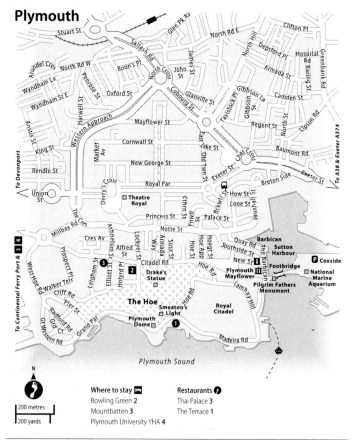

Plymouth

Where to stay 🛏
Bowling Green 2
Mountbatten 3
Plymouth University YHA 4

Restaurants 🍴
Thai Palace 3
The Terrace 1

beyond the Regency café. But not as surely as the former Eddystone lighthouse, **Smeaton's Light**, with its interactive exhibition on the history of the Hoe inside. Next door is the **Plymouth Dome** a former tourist attraction, closed in 2006, but given a new lease of life in January 2013 with the opening of the **Rhodes @ The Dome** restaurant. In the centre of the city, **St Andrew's Church** was badly bombed, but its restored windows by John Piper repay a visit. Dominating the Hoe and the city as a whole, the **Royal Citadel** ① *T01752-266030, www.english-heritage.org.uk, guided tours Mar-Oct, £5, child £4,* was built in the 17th century to defend the coast against the Dutch, and is still used by the military today.

Otherwise, the main attractions are clustered around the **Barbican**, from where the Pilgrim Fathers set sail in 1620, commemorated by a dinky little Greek arch, erected in 1934. Here skippers tout for trade like market criers for boat trips round the Sound. The **Plymouth Mayflower Museum** ① *The Barbican, T01752-306330, Apr-Oct Mon-Sat 0930-1700, Sun 1030-1600, Nov-Mar Mon-Fri 0930-1700, Sat 1030-1600 (last admission 30 mins before closing), £2, under-16s £1, family £5,* is an illustrated account of the city's maritime history on three floors, with excellent views over the old harbour from the top. A short film, model ships (of the *Mayflower* and *Golden Hind*), a treasure chest, Jacobean pottery and interactive graphic panels are among the things on display.

On Coxside, across a swing bridge (access possible daily 0730-2000) and lock gate from the Barbican, in a large glass-front building, is the city's lottery-funded asset, one of the best and certainly the biggest, aquariums in the country. The **National Marine Aquarium** ① *information line T0844-893 7938, www.national-aquarium.co.uk, Apr-Sep daily 1000-1800, Oct-Mar daily 1000-1700, £12.75, under-16s £8.75, concessions £10.50, family £37, tickets for 4D cinema £2.50,* boasts Europe's deepest fish tank, holding two and a half million litres of water, and home to an enormous number of fish, including sharks and seahorses. Various other water-based habitats are also displayed, from the Dartmoor stream to offshore reefs, and at feeding time the excitement is palpable.

Dartmoor → *For listings, see pages 45-47.*

The last wilderness in the country, a mineral-rich moorland 1500 ft above sea level, the largest expanse of granite upland in the country, the biggest open space in the south of England, Dartmoor is about 200 bleak and lonely square miles between Plymouth and Exeter, the source of the Dart, the Tavy, the Taw, the Plym and the Teign rivers. It's a chilling landscape is surrounded by sweet little villages nestling in green valleys, very different though from Exmoor, its little neighbour to the north. Dartmoor's most famous characteristic – along with Her Majesty's prison, the ghosts, bogs and 'letterboxes' – are its distinctive Tors, stumpy granite towers left behind during the last Ice Age.

Okehampton

Okehampton, a solid-looking place, is the main town on the north of the moor, 24 miles west of Exeter on the A30. **All Saints** parish church stands in the middle of the High St, and the ruins of a Norman castle can be found on its western outskirts, but the town has never been prosperous enough to build a market place. Next door to the TIC, an understanding of the way life was once led on the moor can be gained at the **Museum of Dartmoor Life** ① *West St, T01837-52295, www.museumofdartmoorlife.eclipse.co.uk.*

Apr-Oct Mon-Fri 1015-1615 Sat 1015-1300, Nov-mid Dec Mon-Sat 1100-1500. It has the usual information panels, artefacts and sound recordings and also a working waterwheel, in a Georgian mill.

Northeast Dartmoor

Okehampton is also an army town, with a large base on the edge of the Okehampton Common, servicing the **Ministry of Defence firing ranges** that occupy most of northeastern Dartmoor. These desolate restricted areas provide some of the very best yomping country. They are always accessible in the summer and in fact very rarely closed for live firing (contact the free information line above to check). **Yes Tor**, the highest point in the National Park, is one of the most popular destinations for a serious ramble. Not far away is the **source of the Dart** and several other rivers, **Cranmere Pool**, a notorious bog in one of the most remote and inaccessible stretches of the moor. This was also where the first 'letterbox' was placed by James Perrott of Chagford in 1854. The rolling half-wooded hills east of here, strung with stone walls and beech hedges, could hardly be a greater contrast to the open moor. Buffalo roam, within their enclosures of course, near **Cheriton Bishop**, and just to the south, an Edwardian cornershop baron, Julius Drew, founder of Home and Colonial Stores, discovered his ancestral roots. **Castle Drogo** ① *Drewsteignton, T01647-433306, early Mar-Oct daily 1100-1700, garden open daily Mar-Oct 1000-dusk, Nov-Feb 1100-1600, £8.70, under-16s £4.30, gardens and grounds only £5.50, under-16s £3,*

was the result, disappointingly small because unfinished when building work stopped in 1930, but remarkable for being an early-20th-century mock-medieval castle of solid granite with an extremely comfortable fully electrified country house inside. Lutyens was also responsible for the interior, adding amazing Italian glass chandeliers (carefully adapted to carry electric bulbs instead of candles) in the elegant green-panelled drawing room and a very complicated shower system in the bathroom. Outside there are great views over the surrounding woodland, a beautiful rose garden and a large circular croquet lawn (which can be used on application to reception) surrounded for privacy by a thick green hedge and some bright red benches.

Moretonhampstead, 3 miles southeast, is an attractive stone-built village, the 'Gateway to the High Moor' and indeed easily the most scenic approach to the National Park from the east and Exeter on the B3212. Along with the slightly more-out-of-the-way **Chagford**, its neighbour 3 miles to the northwest, these two large unspoiled villages are the last outposts of refined civilization before the moor begins. Moretonhampstead has more pubs, some interesting 17th-century arcaded granite almshouses and a church in a glorious position, its 15th-century tower visible for miles around. Chagford is slightly smarter, tucked away down leafy lanes. It has a popular open-air swimming pool and walks up to the pine wooded Fenworthy Reservoir on the edge of the High Moor.

The Moor

One of the most popular National Parks, and one of the earliest to be given that status, in 1951, walking is the way most people choose to enjoy Dartmoor. Free-range rambling on foot, preferably well-equipped with a good map and hiking boots, covers almost half its area (see page 46). The blanket bog, upland oakwood, caves and mines are natural habitats of tremendous ecological significance, home to a huge variety of flora and fauna, many almost invisible, including endangered species like the southern damselfly, marsh fritillary butterfly and blue ground beetle. The landscape is also amazingly rich in archaeological remains.

From Moretonhampstead the B3212 continues its lonely way southwest on to the moor itself. A tin rush occurred in the middle of the 12th century along this road, which is famously haunted by the 'hairy hands'. They suddenly grab motorbike handlebars and car steering wheels, so it's best not to exceed the 40 mph speed limit. Two miles past the **Miniature Pony Centre**, a haven for the diminutive Dartmoor breed, a small road on the left leads to **Grimspound**, one of the finest remains of a Bronze Age settlement in the country. The places where 24 huts would have stood can be seen, in a 4-acre enclosure surrounded by a low stone wall. The site can usefully be compared with the gravemounds near Chagford at Shoveldown and especially the other Bronze Age settlement at Merrivale (see below), which also has some impressive standing stones.

The B3212 rolls on over the bare land to **Postbridge** (3 miles), passing the isolated **Warren House Inn**, the third highest pub in England; see page 46. On the distant moors opposite, four walled enclosures in the shapes of a suit of playing cards were apparently dropped by a certain Jan Reynolds riding with the Devil. Postbridge is a tiny one-horse town, distinguished by its impressive 13th-century granite clapper bridge. A left turn here leads to the hamlet of **Bellever**, a good jumping-off point for walks along the East Dart river.

Three miles further on, the tree-clad settlement of **Two Bridges** is the crossroads at the heart of the High Moor on the West Dart. Not much to look at, although the smart **Two Bridges Hotel** provides congenial refreshments. A left turn onto the B3357 runs the 4 miles into **Dartmeet**, a delightful but very popular spot where the East and West Dart rivers come together, surrounded by the extensive **Dart Valley Nature Reserve**. A choice of small roads beyond leads either to Buckland in the Moor, where the 10 commandments are inscribed on a rock high above the sinful cluster of thatched cottages beside the river, or to Widecombe-in-the-Moor.

Widecombe-in-the-Moor has been immortalized in Devon's anthem *Tom Pearce*, who has a grey mare (of ghostly origin) that's required to reach Widecombe Fair with "Bill Brewer, Jan Stewer, Peter Gurney, Peter Davey, Dan'l Whiddon, Harry Hawke, old Uncle Tom Cobleigh and all!" It's no surprise then that this is the most popular village in Dartmoor. A green and very picturesque oasis, its beautiful Perpendicular church tower is a reassuring landmark seen across the eastern moor. The Devil had a hand in this too, apparently, pulling it down one stormy night in 1638, killing four people and injuring others. A poem in the church by the local schoolmaster at the time records the event. Outside, **Church House** (NT) is a quaint 16th-century building that has been a brewhouse, almshouse and is now the village hall.

Back on the B3212 at Two Bridges, the road continues for a mile and a half into **Princetown**, the grey, hard-bitten and gloomy capital of the moor, where the main National Park Information Centre is based, before carrying on to **Yelverton**. The atmosphere in Princetown emanates entirely from the **prison** and its situation, constructed in 1809 by French prisoners of war, out of solid granite, and used as an overflow for the prison hulks in Plymouth Sound during the war with America. It became a convict prison in the mid-19th century, and still houses about 700 low-risk criminals. There's a small **museum** ① *T01822-322130, www.dartmoor-prison.co.uk, year round Mon-Sat 0930-1230, 1330-1630, Fri and Sat 0930-1230, 1330-1600 (last admission 30 mins before closing), £3, under-18s £2, family £9*, on its history, in the old stables, with chain-gang leg-irons and a mock-up cell, which hardly does much to lift the spirits.

Tavistock to Lydford

The B3357 from Two Bridges bypasses Princetown on its way to Tavistock, over the boulder-strewn, grassy landscape, past mossy stone walls and **Merrivale**, with its standing stones, as well as abandoned tin mines. These may also have extracted tungsten, lead, silver, sulphur, manganese, copper, or zinc. Tavistock, is a grey-stone and crennellated town, with an excellent **Pannier Market** (selling some very fine cheeses) and a dignified air. Seven miles up the road back towards Okehampton, Lydford is a popular beauty spot with a castle and the famous **gorge** ① *(NT), T01822-820320, Apr-Sep daily 1000-1700, Oct-Mar daily 1000-1600, £6.05, child £3.05, family £15.25.* A circular walk leads down the more than mile-long ravine through oak woods to the **White Lady**, a 30-m-high waterfall and the whirlpool at the bottom called the Devil's Cauldron.

Plymouth and Dartmoor listings

For hotel and restaurant price codes and other relevant information, see pages 9-13.

🛏 Where to stay

Plymouth *p39, map p40*

££ Bowling Green Hotel, 9-10 Osborne Pl, Lockyer St, The Hoe, T01752-209090, www.thebowlinggreenplymouth.com. A friendly, family-run hotel with comfortably furnished rooms looking over the Hoe.

££ Mountbatten Hotel, 52 Exmouth Rd, Stoke, T01752-484660, www.hotel mountbatten.co.uk. A little way out of town toward the Tor ferry, a quiet family-run Victorian guesthouse near Devonport station.

££ Plymouth University YHA, Gibbon St, T01752-588599. A choice of single and double en suite rooms are available in the university's halls of residence from the last week of Jun until the beginning of Sep.

Dartmoor *p41*

££££ Gidleigh Park, Chagford, T01647-432367, www.gidleigh.com. Internationally renowned mock-Tudor country house boutique hotel, with a range of rooms (from spa suites and family loft suites to dog-friendly rooms) and a restaurant run by Michelin Star head chef Michael Caines.

££££-£££ The Horn of Plenty, Gulworthy, Tavistock, T01822-832528, www.thehornofplenty.co.uk. Great views over the Tamar valley and inventive food.

£££ Eastwrey Barton, Lustleigh, T01647-277338, www.eastwreybarton.co.uk. B&B in a Georgian country house with 5 luxurious en suite rooms.

£££-££ Lydgate House, Postbridge, T01822-880209, www.lydgatehouse.co.uk. In a superb location beside the East Dart River, a small award-winning non-smoking country house hotel with 7 rooms (bathroom en suite).

££ Castle Inn, Lydford, near Oakhampton, T01822-820241. www.castleinndartmoor.co.uk. Close to the White Lady waterfall and the Devil's Cauldron, local cheeses and home-made soups on the menu.

££ Cherry Brook Hotel, Two Bridges, T01822-880260, thecherrybrook.co.uk. Right in the middle of the moor, between Two Bridges and Postbridge, also with 7 cosy bedrooms (bathroom en suite).

££ Church House Inn, Holne, near Ashburton, T01364-631208, www.dartmoorchurchhouseinn.co.uk. Organic food on the menu and views over the moor from a good pub in the middle of a small village. Comfortable rooms.

££ Higher Venton Farm, Widecombe, T01364-621235, www.ventonfarm.com, with 2 double rooms, 1 twin, in a thatched longhouse, as well as 2 double rooms next door.

£ YHA Dartmoor, near Postbridge, T0845-371 9622, www.yha.org.uk Right in the middle of the moor, with 38 beds.

£ YHA Okehampton Bracken Tor, Saxongate, T0844-293 0555, www.yha.org.uk. Basic but comfortable accommodation in grounds of 4 acres with access to a network of walking and cycling trails.

Self-catering

£££ Holne Chase Holiday Cottages, Two Bridges Rd, Ashburton, T01747-828170, www.holne-chase.co.uk. Luxury dog-friendly self-catering cottages with excellent pony riding and fishing nearby.

Camping

Cockingford Farm, Widecombe in the Moor, T01364-621258. In a wooded valley with a stream, campfires allowed. Pitches cost £8 a night for 2 adults.

£ **YHA Camping Barns**, T0800-0191 700, www.yha.org.uk. at Runnage (2, on a working farm near Bellever Forest and the River Dart), at Great Hound Tor (near Manator, and Widecombe, in a former farmhouse with 2 upstairs sleeping galleries) and at the Fox and Hounds (near Lydford, with a pub next door).

🍴 Restaurants

Plymouth p39, map p40
££ Thai Palace, 3 Eliot St, The Hoe, T01752-255770, www.thaipalace.co.uk. An efficient, tasty Thai restaurant.
£ The Terrace, The Hoe, T01752-603533, www.theterracecafebar.co.uk. Lovely views of Plymouth Sound.

Dartmoor p41
££ Rugglestone Inn, Widecombe-in- the-Moor, T01364-621327, www.rugglestoneinn.co.uk. Open fires and stone floors as well as home-cooked food, real ales and lots of dogs.

🍺 Pubs, bars and clubs

Dartmoor p41
The Cleave, Lustleigh, T01647-277223, thecleavelustleigh.com. Thatched pub with cottage garden on the edge of Dartmoor.
Drew Arms, Drewstaignton, T01647-281224, www.thedrewarms.co.uk. A fine old pub where they still pass beers through the hatch.
Peter Tavy Inn, T01822-810348, www.petertavyinn.com, near Tavistock, convenient for walks onto the moor.
The Rock, Haytor Vale, T01364-661305, www.rock-inn.co.uk. Fine dining a la carte restaurant and 9 comfortable guest rooms.
Warren House Inn, Postbridge, T01822-880208, www.warrenhouseinn.co.uk. Has had a fire burning in the grate continually since 1845. Famous for its Warrener's Pie (rabbit feast), it's the third highest pub in England, 1425 ft above sea level, close to the King's Oven prehistoric entrance grave.

⛰ What to do

Dartmoor p41
Cycling
The 11-mile **Granite Way** on an old railway line runs from Okehampton to Lydford, part of the Devon Coast to Coast Cycleway.
Devon Cycle Hire, Sourton Down, Okehampton, T01837-861141, www.devoncyclehire.co.uk.
Tavistock Cycles, Paddons Row, Brook St, Tavistock, T01822-617630, www.tavistockcycles.co.uk. Cycle hire.

Horse riding
Shilstone Rock Stud, near Widecombe-in-the-Moor, T01362-621281, www.dartmoorstables.com.

Letterboxing
Letterbox 100 Club, 1 Dryfield, Exminster, Exeter, T01392-832768, www.letterboxingondartmoor.co.uk. Membership available after collecting 100 stamps.

Swimming
Open-air swimming pool, Chagford, T01647-432929, www.chagfordpool.co.uk. May-Sep daily 1400-1900.

Walking
Rambler's Association (Devon), www.devonramblers.org.uk.

🚌 Transport

Plymouth p39, map p40
Boat
Brittany Ferries, T0871-244 0744, www.brittany-ferries.co.uk, to and from **Santander, St Malo** and **Roscoff** embark and arrive at Millbay Ferry Port, a mile and a half west of the city centre and the Barbican, overlooked by the West Hoe. (Regular bus service via the city centre to the train station.)
Cremyll Pedestrian Ferry, T07746-199508,

www.cremyll-ferry.co.uk, operates from Admiral's Hard (off Durnford St, Stonehouse) to **Mount Edgcumbe Park** in Cornwall. A ferry timetable may be purchased at the Cremyll Tollgate. **Plymouth Boat Trips**, T01752-253153, www.plymouth boattrips.co.uk, operate boat trips from Plymouth Barbican, as well as a ferry service to Cawsand and Kingsand on Cornwall's Rame Peninsula. The **Torpoint Ferry**,T01752-812233, www.tamar crossings.org.uk, is a regular and frequent car and pedestrian ferry service operating between Torpoint and **Devonport**.

Car
Avis, 20 Commercial Rd, Coxside, Cattedown, T08445-446090.
Thrifty, 15 Sutton Rd, T01752-207207.

Taxi
Central Taxis, Cumberland St, T01752-363636.
Tower Cabs, 138 North Rd East, T01752-252525, www.towercabs.com.

Train
Plymouth Railway Station is on the main London-Penzance railway line. **First Great Western** provide a frequent service throughout the day and an overnight sleeper to **London Paddington** while **Virgin Trains** operate through cross-country services to major cities in the **Midlands**, the **North of England** and **Scotland**. First Great Western also operate the Tamar Valley Line to destinations such as **Gunnislake**, **Callington**, **Cotehele House**, **Morwellham Quay**. These services operate from Devonport, Dockyard, Keyham and St Budeaux stations as well as Plymouth station. On Sun in the summer, special trains along the Tamar Valley Line link with a planned network of buses at Gunnislake to give access to **Dartmoor** and beyond. For details of the Tamar Valley Line in general www.carfreedaysout.com.

ⓘ Directory

Plymouth *p39, map p40*
Medical facilities Derriford Hospital, Derriford Rd, Crownhill, T01752-202082/0845-155 81553.

North Devon Coast

Apart from the tourist hotspots at the seaside resort of Ilfracombe and pickled cliffside fishing village of Clovelly, the North Devon Coast just about continues to remain unspoiled although hardly undiscovered. It's a wonderland of sweeping sands, crumbling cliffs, tiny roads and wild rocky headlands. Ilfracombe gives a good taste of what's in store with its crazy coastal scenery, while Woolacombe and Croyde are the original English surfers' beaches. Barnstaple is the staid and slightly bewildered market town at the heart of the region, wondering how to keep up with arty Bideford and its little neighbour Appledore. It's a two-hour boat trip from Ilfracombe or Bideford to get to Lundy Island, a three-mile chunk of granite rising from the Bristol Channel, 11 miles north of Hartland Point as the gull flies. Beyond Clovelly, the Hartland peninsula is one of the best places in Britain to get lost in. Head any way towards the setting sun and you'll end up on a dramatic nub of granite butting the Atlantic.

Visiting the North Devon Coast

Getting there
The Tarka Line, run by **First Great Western**, T08457-000125, www.firstgreat western.co.uk, www.carfreedaysout.com/tarka, covers 39 exceptionally scenic miles between Exeter and Barnstaple, every couple of hrs or so, taking just over an hr, and passing through Crediton and small villages like Umberleigh, Eggesford, Morchard Road, Copplestone and Newton St Cyres en route. **National Rail Enquiries**, T08457-484950, www.nationalrail.co.uk. By road, the quickest way of reaching Barnstaple, Bideford and the north coast between Lynton and Ilfracombe is via junction 27 on the M5 to Tiverton and then the A361. The A39 is a beautiful but congested route from Bridgwater (junction 24 on the M5). Barnstaple is about 4 hours from London by car by the former route, about 5 by the latter. ▸▸ *See Transport, page 54.*

Getting around
Barnstaple is the hub of the bus network in the area, with regular services to Ilfracombe and Bideford, fewer out to Hartland. Many of the buses are run by **First** in Devon, T0845-600 1420, www.firstgroup.com/ukbus/devon_cornwall. Interactive bus maps and guides can be found at **Journey Devon**, www.journeydevon.info. Cycling is a very good option round the coast and in Hartland.

Tourist information
Barnstaple TIC ① *The Square, T01271-375000, www.staynorthdevon.co.uk.* **Bideford TIC** ① *The Quay, Kingsley Rd, T01237-477676.* *Ilfracombe TIC, The Seafront, T01271-863001, www.visitilfracombe.co.uk.* **Lynton TIC** ① *The Town Hall, Lee Rd, T01598-752225, www.lynton-ynmouth-tourism.co.uk.* **Woolacombe TIC** ① *The Esplanade, T01271-870553, www.woolacombetourism.co.uk.*

Lynton to Barnstaple → *For listings, see pages 53-54.*

From the Valley of the Rocks, a mile west of Lynton, the **South West Coast Path** winds past the leafy combes and secret coves of Woody Bay towards the beauty spot of **Heddon's Mouth**, full of large round pebbles, some way below the peaceful wooded seclusion of the **Hunter's Inn**. Four miles further west, the overgrown village of **Combe Martin** nestles in a valley with a view of the sea, a popular family seaside spot where silver was once mined. The kids might well enjoy a day at **Watermouth Castle** ① *T01271-867474, www.watermouthcastle.com, Easter-Oct phone for times, £13.25, under-13s £11.25, under 92 cm free*, a little toy fort of a house with an adventure theme park attached just up the hill near the pretty village of Berrynarbor. Nearby on the coast, **Watermouth Cove**, where Enid Blyton set some of her Famous Five stories, is a charming sheltered little cove with a safe beach.

Ilfracombe and around

A couple of miles to the west, Ilfracombe, the largest, busiest and most chaotically situated resort on the North Devon Coast, spreads itself out over a confusion of low cliffs, beaches and bays looking out to sea. A Victorian and Edwardian resort of considerable note, today, with its bluffs, hidden beaches and big seabirds, it looks like the perfect setting for a B-movie. Carefully tended allotment gardens stretch up quiet wooded slopes on the approach, before the town suddenly gets into its stride on the bustling narrow High Street, surrounded on all sides by the crumbling Victorian boomtown architecture that gives the place its faded English charm. A walk up bald **Capstone Hill** on the seafront beyond the pepperpot cones of the Landmark Theatre will clear the head and give uninterrupted views of the town's peculiar layout behind its old Promenade, little harbour and the sea.

The holiday spirit is strong here in summer, and also more innocent than the seaside resorts in south Devon. Old-timers looking to escape the crush for more tranquility head for the old Quay and boat trips round the bay or out to Lundy Island (see below) on *MS Oldenburg* (tickets from TIC or the office on Ilfracombe pier T01271-863636), families make for the rockpools on the **Tunnel Beaches**, gaining access thanks to Welsh miners who burrowed through the cliffs from the Bath House in the late 19th century. The whole town goes mad for old times during the **Victorian Celebrations** in the middle of June, dressing up in crinolines and bonnets. **Ilfracombe Museum** ① *T01271-863541, www.ilfracombemuseum.co.uk, Apr-Oct daily 1000-1700, Nov-Mar Tue-Fri 1000-1300, £3, concessions £2.50, under-16s free*, close to the Landmark Theatre, is a collector's paradise, an extraordinary array of odds and ends from days gone by in an old laundry house. As well as a Lundy Island display, here be clocks, hats, bells, bats, shells, chandlery as well as a pickled two-faced kitten, a two-headed gosling and a four-legged chicken in the natural history section.

The very fine **Torrs Walk** zigzags through impressive coastal scenery (NT) west of Ilfracombe to the much smaller resort at **Lee**, famous for its fuschias and also the sweet secluded Lee Bay, reached via the Lee Abbey Toll road (£1 cars).

Nearby, working Collie dogs going head-to-head with woolly sheep while falconry action rages overhead can be enjoyed near the village of **Mortehoe** at the **Woolacombe Working Sheepdog and Falconry** ① *Borough Farm, T01271-870056, www.borough*

farm.co.uk, Wed from late May at 1800, £5, child £2.50, under-5s free. Lambing open days and shepherding experiences are also available.

Woolacombe

Round the promontory of Bull Point and Rockham Bay, Woolacombe's sandy beach stretches for almost 3 miles south. Half close your eyes and the breakers heading onto the sweep of the bay could almost be pounding on Laguna Beach. Very popular with surfers as well – the first full-time surf hut in England was established here in the 60s – who head for the Putsborough end of the beach, it never seems that crowded even though surrounded by holiday homes and camping parks spread around the **Bay Hotel**. Round the promontory of Baggy Point to the south, little **Croyde Bay** is the place the surfers go when Woolacombe won't deliver.

Barnstaple

Nine miles east of Croyde, past the 4-mile wide expanse of Saunton Sands, Barnstaple is the region's market town, a pleasant enough place spoiled by too much traffic, at the head of the Taw Estuary. With an ancient history stretching back to the foundation of Wessex, in the ninth century it was the most westerly port in Alfred's kingdom and continued to prosper after being fortified by the Normans and later traded with the Americas. The impressive remains of its role as a marketplace can be seen in the centre of town at the **Pannier Market** and along Butcher's Row, although the shops and markets themselves are a bit tired. Queen Anne's Walk, an 18th-century colonnade housing a heritage centre complete with laughable costumed mannequins, is along the riverside on The Strand, near the old Castle Quay. There's not much else to keep visitors here long, most using the town as a convenient base for exploring the area inland and along the coast.

Lundy Island → *For listings, see pages 53-54.*

From both Bideford and Ilfracombe boats run out to Lundy Island, famous for its occasional glimpses of puffins but also a day trip for a walk. Boats also go to Lundy from Clovelly, but most visitors are content to struggle up and down its impossibly photogenic main street, awestruck by how quaint a singularly sited fishing village in private hands can be.

Visiting Lundy Island

Getting there Departures on *MS Oldenburg* March to December various days, T01271-863636, www.lundyisland.co.uk/sailing, from Bideford usually between 0800 and 1000, from Ilfracombe usually 1000, arriving back at between 1830 and 2000. Sailing time just under 2 hours. Tickets cost £35 day return, £18 under-16s, £6 under-4s, family £80. Period return £62, under-16s £30.50. Also the *Jessica Hettie* sails April to October from Clovelly £35, under-16s £25 return, T01237- 431405, www.clovelly-charters.ukf.net.

Tourist information Lundy Shore Office ① *The Quay, Bideford, T01237-470422; Lundy Island T01237-863636, www.lundyisland.co.uk.* Short stays available on the island late March to October in a range of historic buildings, including a 13th-century castle,

lighthouse, Georgian villa and fisherman's chalet; book through the **Landmark Trust**
ⓘ *Shottesbrooke, Maidenhead, Berkshire, T01628-825925, www.landmarktrust.org.uk.*

Places on Lundy Island

A flattened granite outcrop 3 miles long and half a mile wide, 10 miles north of the Devon
coast, windswept Lundy Island sits in the middle of the Bristol Channel like a giant
petrified whale. Boats run out to it regularly in summer from Ilfracombe, Bideford and
Clovelly. Inhabited by about 30 people, as well as lots of seabirds, rabbits, Soay sheep and
a herd of Sika deer, it's owned by the National Trust and run by the Landmark Trust, who
maintain and let the small amount of delightful but quite pricey self-catering and B&B
accommodation. The island's own ship, *MS Oldenburg*, carrying its capacity of 267
passengers in the summer, makes regular day trips most months of the year. On arrival at
the jetty on the very southern tip of the island, a fairly steep climb up past the lighthouse
arrives at the main settlement, gathered around the **Marisco Tavern** (see page 53). Day
trippers usually have about 5 or 6 hours to spend on the island: admiring the strange rocks
on the coastline, looking hard for puffins (only a good idea in June when these colourful
burrowing birds breed on the west coast) and just enjoying the fresh air. The island has a
long history of piracy and later, comfortable respectability, which it pretty much still
maintains thanks to the restrictions on access. No dogs are allowed either.

Bideford to Hartland → *For listings, see pages 53-54.*

Seven miles southwest of Barnstaple is its great maritime rival, Bideford. Marginally more
picturesque, and smaller, it was described by local novelist Charles 'Water Babies'
Kingsley as the "the little white town". It once owed its prosperity to its 27-arch medieval
bridge over the River Torridge. Walter Raleigh first landed tobacco here. Trips to Lundy
(see above) can be taken aboard *MS Oldenburg*, while next door to Victoria Park is the
Burton Art Gallery ⓘ *Kingsley Rd, T01237-471455, www.burtonartgallery.co.uk, Mon-Sat
1000-1600, Sun 1100-1600,* an interesting space for permanent and temporary
exhibitions, with a section on Bideford's heritage and tourist information.

Further upriver, the little fishing village of **Appledore** is a surprising delight: a kind of
mini St Ives in north Devon, with an arty but unpretentious atmosphere, its pretty little
harbour feeding small boats into the mouth of the Torridge where it meets the Taw. On
the opposite bank, near Instow, **Tapeley Park Gardens** ⓘ *T01271-860528,
www.tapeleygardens.com, Easter-Oct Sun-Fri 1000-1700, £5, under-16s £3, concessions
£4,* are an Italian garden created by the architect Sir John Belcher in the 19th century,
with a walled vegetable garden, curious shell grotto, ornamental terraces lined with
lavender and fuschia, a variety of other gardens and a lake surrounded by ancient
evergreens. There are beautiful views over the estuary on the walk to a labyrinth and
monument too.

Clovelly, 12 miles west of Bideford on the A39, must be one of the most photographed
villages in Britain. A privately owned and immaculately preserved fishing village that
tumbles down a steep gorge on a wooded hill to a tiny harbour, it's a rivulet of cobbles,
dinky cottages, and tearooms trickling between gently crumbling russet cliffs. Really only
for the very sweet-toothed, it nonetheless has to be seen to be believed. And thousands
do want to do just that, despite the entry fee (£6.50, child £4, family £17) charged at the

Clovelly Visitor Centre ① *T01237-431781, www.clovelly.co.uk, daily 0930-1730*, at the top of the hill. After the crowds have toiled up and down the single main street, 'up-along' and 'down-along' as it's called, and headed home, the **Red Lion Hotel** right on the tiny quayside really comes into its own, as do the peaceful walks along the cliffs and the Hobby Road. Despite being a museum, Clovelly is still alive, with a lifeboat station, fishing and boating trips to Lundy, donkeys dragging provisions or carrying children up and down, residents and visitors enjoying the two hotels in the evenings. The Long Walk leads up to **Clovelly Court**, the home of the Rous family who own the place, with a fine Victorian **kitchen garden** ① *year round 1000-1600, admission included in entry to village*. From here too, a romantic clifftop walk leads through tangled old woods to **The Lookout** with glimpses of the sea below from the ornate **Angel's Wings** shelter and **Gallantry Bower**, the remains of a Bronze Age bowl barrow.

About 7 miles south of Clovelly, near the village of West Putford, the **Gnome Reserve** ① *T01409-241435, www.gnomereserve.co.uk, late Mar-Oct daily 1000-1800, £3.75, under-16s £3.25*, is an epiphany to little people made of clay. More than 1,000 of the blessed garden ornaments are dotted around 2 acres of beech woodland. Visitors get a gnome hat to get into the spirit, and there's also a labelled wild flower garden.

West of Clovelly, some of England's most beautiful and rugged coastal and inland scenery stretches out towards **Hartland Point**. The town of Hartland itself seems to be pretty much stuck in another era, a peaceful enclave of whitewashed houses with lead roofs. A mile to the west, in a beautiful sheltered valley about a mile from the rugged Atlantic coast, **Hartland Abbey** ① *T01237-441496, www.hartlandabbey.com, Apr-Sep Sun-Thu, bank holidays 1400-1700 (last entry 1630), gardens only 11.30-1700, £10.50, under-15s £4, family £25*, is an unexpected oasis of ordered calm. The mock-medieval house stands on the site of an Augustinian priory founded in the mid-12th century and the last to be dissolved, given by Henry VIII to his wine keeper. A lovely mile-long wooded walk leads down to the sea.

North Devon Coast listings

For hotel and restaurant price codes and other relevant information, see pages 9-13.

🛏 Where to stay

Lynton to Barnstaple *p49*

££££ Saunton Sands Hotel, near Braunton, T01271-890212, www.sauntonsands.co.uk. Lively hotel with smallish rooms but 4-star facilities, including a heated outdoor pool, health club, babysitting and a private path to the beach, with magnificent views over the sands from its terrace.

££ Broomhill Art Hotel, Muddiford, near Barnstaple, T01271-850262, www.broomhillart.co.uk. Small country house hotel with a heated swimming pool, in a wooded valley with a sculpture park. Dog friendly.

££ Humes Farm Cottage, Bradiford, near Barnstaple, T01271-345039, www.humesfarm.co.uk. Beautifully restored self-catering cottages sleeping 4 or 5 in a quiet out-of-the-way village, just outside Barnstaple towards Braunton.

££ Huxtable Farm, West Buckland, near Barnstaple, T01598-760254, www.huxtablefarm.co.uk. 16th-century working farmhouse 5 miles east of Barnstaple, with local produce on the table.

££ Lyncott House, 56 St Brannock's Rd, Ilfracombe, T01271-862425, www.lyncotthouse.co.uk. Comfortable Victorian guesthouse close to Bicclescombe gardens and a 15-min walk to the harbour.

Bideford to Hartland *p51*

£££ Hartland Quay Hotel, Hartland, T01 237-441218, www.hartlandquayhotel.co.uk. Sweet family-run hotel in a spectacular position overlooking the spume-ridden waves.

£££ Red Lion Hotel, Clovelly, T01237-431781, www.clovelly.co.uk.

Comfortable accommodation right by the harbour, with good food.

££ Golden Park, Hartland, near Bideford, T01237-441254, www.goldenpark.co.uk. 17th-century farmhouse B&B with sea views, a walled garden and 3 bedrooms with en suite bathrooms.

££ Ocean Backpackers, 29 St James Pl, Ilfracombe, T01271-867835, www.oceanbackpackers.co.uk. 46-bed hostel with en suite dorms, double and family rooms, a short stroll from the harbour and main bus station.

£ Camping Barn at Mullacott Farm, Ilfracombe, bookings T0800-019 1700. Recently renovated accommodation in some former stables.

🍴 Restaurants

Lynton to Barnstaple *p49*

££ Hunters Inn, Heddon's Mouth, near Parracombe, T01598-763230, www.thehuntersinn.net. A good place for a pub lunch in a secluded wooded spot with peacocks roaming in the gardens.

££ Pyne Arms, East Down, near Barnstaple, T01271-850055, www.pynearms.co.uk . Flower-filled tubs in the garden and good food on the table in a low-ceilinged pub.

Lundy Island *p50*

££ Marisco Tavern, Lundy, T01237-431831. The only pub on the island, and luckily it's a good one, with a garden and traditional filling pub grub, ideal after a bracing day hunting puffins. Booking office for Lundy Island: T01237-470074.

⛰ What to do

Lynton to Barnstaple *p49*
Horseriding
Woolacombe Riding Stables, Eastacott Farm, T01271-870260, www.woolacombe-ridingstables.co.uk.

Surfing

Surf South West, Croyde Bay,
T01271-890400, www.surfsouthwest.com.
Apr-Oct daily 1030-1230, 1330-1530. Half day
£32, full day £62, weekend (3 lessons) £90.

 Transport

Bideford to Hartland *p51*
Bicycle
Bideford Bicycle Hire, Torrington St, East
the Water, Bideford, T01237-424123,
www.bidefordbicyclehire.co.uk. £11 full day.
Torrington Cycle Hire, The Station,
Torrington, T01805-622633, www.torrington
cyclehire.co.uk. £11.50 full day.

Contents

Footprint features

Cornwall

England's far southwestern corner, Cornwall is as Celtic as Brittany. A sainted, holy place, it was Christian long before the rest of England, buzzing with missionaries from Ireland and Wales, and today still possesses a proudly independent spirit, a significant and surprisingly serious separatist movement mustering under its black and white banner and nurturing the Cornish language. But it also has the lowest income per capita in the country, and in parts remains severely depressed, something which the yearly influx of holidaymakers, most heading west determinedly for the sea, only goes some way towards alleviating. Quite apart from the instability of the tourist trade generally, the popularity of certain areas of the peninsula with visitors, especially in July and August, threatens to rob them of any magic.

The North Cornish Coast has the busiest beachlife and harbours: the Arthurian mysteries of Tintagel, the gourmet's haven at Padstow on the Camel estuary, and Newquay, the full-on surf capital of the UK. In the middle of the county squats the bare granite wastes of Bodmin Moor, sliced in half by the A30, but surrounded by amazingly luxuriant gardens. Now easily the most famous of them is the Eden Project, an extraordinary 21st-century redevelopment of a disused clay pit into a spectacular greenhouse. The south coast nearby is worth exploring for its more traditional gardens and tiny little harbour villages.

Further west, Falmouth and the Lizard repay a visit for their mild climate and coastal scenery. Arty St Ives sets the tone for the Penwith Peninsula, which peters out at Land's End with a notorious visitor attraction hailing the 'Relentless Sea'. Some 30 miles beyond, the Isles of Scilly are a delightful little subtropical archipelago where our Bronze Age ancestors went to bury their dead in the path of the setting sun.

North Cornish Coast

The continuation of the superb North Devon Coast to the south and west into Cornwall is one of the most spectacular stretches of the South West Coast Path. Sure it's had its fair share of ill-advised developments, bungalows and fixed caravan parks, but the cliffs and beaches between Bude and Newquay keep hikers and surfboarders happy throughout the long season. Bude is the typical north Cornish seaside resort, flanked by wonderful surfing beaches at Sandy Mouth and Widemouth, both better for beginners on the board than overcrowded Newquay to the south. Boscastle is the most picturesque fishing village on the coast, owned by the National Trust like much of the treasured coastline along here, and very busy in summer. Crowds and coaches also make for Tintagel, legendary birthplace of King Arthur, but out of season the dramatic situation of this ruined coastal castle should satisfy the most demanding romantic. On the Camel Estuary, the only large river to meet the sea in north Cornwall, the medieval harbour town of Padstow has been given a new lease of life by TV chef Rick Stein, whose restaurants draw people down from London. And low-cost airfares to Newquay have boosted that resort's already booming reputation for being up for it – surf culture and Ibizan nightlife that is.

Visiting the North Cornish Coast

Getting there

Several airlines fly to **Newquay Cornwall Airport** ① *T01637-860600, www.newquay cornwallairport.com*, including **Air Southwest**, T0870-241 8202, www.airsouth west.com; **BMI Baby**, T0871-224 0224, www.bmibaby.com; **Flybe**, T0871-700 2000, www.flybe.com; **Jet2.com**, T0871-226 1737, www.jet2.com; and **Ryanair**, T0871-246 0000, www.ryanair.com. **Isles of Scilly Travel**, T0845-710 5555, www.ios-travel.co.uk, operates Skybus services to the islands. The airport is located 5 miles outside Newquay town centre, with regular buses between the two. A taxi to the town centre will set you back approximately £15.

First Great Western, T08457-000125, www.firstgreatwestern.co.uk, run direct services between London Paddington and Penzance, taking between five and six hours and calling at Liskeard, Bodmin, Par, St Austell, Truro, Redruth, Camborne, Hayle and St Erth. **National Rail Enquiries**, T08457-484950, www.nationalrail.co.uk.

By road, Hartland Point and the North Cornish Coast remain one of the most remote and inaccessible destinations in the southwest. The only express routes by road involve either the A361 via Barnstaple from the Tiverton exit on the M5, or the A30 and A3079 via Holsworthy, joining the A39 at Bude. Either way will take a good 5 hours from London. Padstow is about 15 miles from the main M5/A30 route, 4 hours from London on a very good day, Newquay a little further on the same route.

National Express, T08717-818178, www.nationalexpress.com, run coaches to Falmouth, Newquay, Penzance, St Austell, St Ives, Truro and most other main centres in Cornwall, with connecting services from Bristol, Birmingham and London.

Getting around

Scenic branch lines, www.greatscenicrailways.com, include St Erth–St Ives, following the shores of the Hayle Estuary and St Ives Bay with stops at Lelant and Carbis Bay; Truro–Falmouth, a half-hourly service linking Perranwell and Penryn; Par–Newquay, a route joining the north and south coasts, and Liskeard–Looe, an hourly service through the Looe Valley.

Buses run to the Eden Project from St Austell station and Helston from Redruth station. First T0845-600 1420, www.firstgroup.com, and **Western Greyhound** T01637-871871, www.westerngreyhound.com, run a good network of buses around the north coast to places like Tintagel and Bude from Truro, Bodmin, Okehampton, Plymouth, and Exeter, but covering any distances will require patience.

Tourist information

Bodmin ⓘ *Shire Hall, Mount Folly, T01208-76616.* **Bude** ⓘ *Crescent Car Park, T01288-354240, www.visitbude.info.* **Lostwithiel** ⓘ *Community Centre, Liddicoat Rd, T01208-872207.* **Newquay TIC** ⓘ *Marcus Hill, T01872-322900, www.visitnewquay.org.* **Padstow TIC** ⓘ *The Red Brick Building, North Quay, Padstow, T01841-533449, www.padstowlive.com, Apr-Oct 0930-1700, Nov-Mar Mon-Fri 0930-1700.* **Tintagel Visitor Centre** ⓘ *T01840-779084, www.visitboscastleandtintagel.com, daily Apr-Oct 1000-1700, Nov-Mar 1030-1600.*

Bude and Boscastle → *For listings, see pages 65-67.*

Morwenstow, the most northerly village in England's most southerly county, lies a mile from the impressive coastal scenery of the **Sharpnose Points**, Higher and Lower. The village itself is immortally associated with one of the Anglican church's most eccentric vicars, the Rev RS Hawker, who tirelessly buried the local shipwrecked dead around his Norman church here (against the custom of burying them on the beach) between 1834 and 1875. A friend of Tennyson, he would retire to Hawker's Hut, a bothy he made for himself on the cliff from ship's timbers, to smoke opium and have visions, after visiting his flock with his pet pig. He also decorated his vicarage with chimneys in the shape of his favourite church towers and erected the figurehead of the wrecked *Caledonia* in the graveyard.

South of Morwenstow, as far as Tintagel, Cornwall's Atlantic coast provides one of the country's finest walks along a particularly inspiring stretch of the **South West Coastal Path**. **Sandy Mouth** beach (NT) gets the ball rolling, a 3-mile-long surfer's delight but easily big enough for everyone to enjoy. At its southern end sits Bude, quite a sweet Regency seaside resort, developed but not ruined, with donkey rides on the prom and peace and quiet only a short walk away. Except that here the Atlantic rages higher and harder than anywhere else in Cornwall, apparently audible up to 10 miles away. The town straddles a little estuary, flanked by superb cliffs, looking out over miles of sand at low tide.

Even more popular with surfers is Widemouth Bay, 3 miles to the south. Pronounced 'Widdymuth' but true enough to its name anyway, it gives a good mile of steady breakers. Widemouth is fairly heavily commercialized though, so those looking for a less rowdy spot press on for 5 miles or so round Dizzard Point to **Crackington Haven** (NT). With a tea

Walks in Cornwall

• **Bedruthan Steps**: 2 miles there and back. Start: Trenance, car park on the B3276. A spectacular section of the South West Coast Path above massive slate cliffs and caves. OS Maps: Explorer 106, Landranger 200.

• **South Cornish Coast**: 2 mile circle. Start: Pencarrow, 4 miles west of Polperro. A walk out on to the dramatic triangular headland, with wide views along the coast east and west. OS Maps: Explorer 107, Landranger 201.

• **North Cornish Coast**: 6 miles one way. Start: Coombe village, 4 miles north of Bude. Nature trails wind through wooded valleys to the coast, and north past Morwenstow to Hennacliff. OS Maps: Explorer 126, Landranger 190.

• **Lizard**: 4 miles one way. Start: Kynance Cove, off the A3083 between Helston and Lizard. A bracing walk along the clifftops to Mullion Cove. Loe pool is another 5 miles further on. OS Maps: Explorer 103, Landranger 203.

shop, beach café, pub and a sandy beach (also with reliable surf) tucked behind the Cambeak headland, the place has also long been a favourite with crusties, campers and alternative types. Even more seclusion can be found just south at the **Strangles**, a lovely beach with no facilities and quite tricky to reach down a 500-ft drop from the cliff top but worth the effort to find weird rock formations and sea arches.

About five miles south, **Boscastle** is a National Trust village that was once a delightful little harbour town and the main point of embarkation for Delabole slate. A bit overwhelmed by tourism these days, nothing can detract from its extraordinary position wedged into the valley of the Valency like a miniature Norwegian fjord. It's worth walking out beyond the pretty thatched riverfront and stone harbour onto the sea slates for the impressive views of the coastline north and south. If the tide is right, near here the blowhole called the **Devil's Bellows** may be rumbling and throwing up spray. A mile or so up the valley, Thomas Hardy worked as a young architect on the tower of the church at **St Juliot's** and turned his experience into material for his novel *A Pair of Blue Eyes*, calling the village Endelstow. Hardy also married the leader of the church choir, Emma Gifford.

Tintagel and around → *For listings, see pages 65-67.*

ⓘ *Tintagel Castle, T01840-770328, www.english-heritage.org.uk. Easter-Oct, daily from 1000, Nov-Easter Sat-Sun 1000-1600. £5.70, concessions £5.10, under-16s £3.40, family £14.80. Special evening events in Jul and Aug. Introductory talks daily during the summer.*

The 4-mile **cliff-top walk** from Boscastle to Tintagel has often been described as one of the finest in England. No surprise that it's popular then, especially as its passes through **Rocky Valley** just north of Tintagel, but in part the sentiment must have something to do with the destination and the peculiar place that Tintagel occupies in the English imagination. Arthur is the name of the game here. The village's single street takes the commercialization of the legendary King to the heights of tack. But then again it can't escape the fact that no one comes here to see the village. The spectacular ruins of the 14th-century cliffside castle and thin neck of land leading out to the 'island' rock are the main event and would be worth a trip even if they weren't believed to be the birthplace of King Arthur. A crumbling battlemented wall runs up the sheer 300-ft headland and on the other side of the chasm, the mystical spot itself, **Arthur's Castle** perched on a rock battered by the sea. This is where his father Uther Pendragon is supposed to have seduced Queen Igraine, with help of the magic of Merlin, whose **Cave** roars in the waves down below. It's also where the tragic lovers Tristan and Isolde are buried, according to the poet Swinburne, just one of the literary greats to have been inspired by Malory's *Morte d'Arthur* and Geoffrey of Monmouth's imaginative 12th-century *History of Britain*, if not by Tintagel itself. In high summer, the popularity of the place and bright sunshine can undermine the mystery, but at any other time the atmosphere seems absolutely appropriate to England's Dark Age warrior king and his gallant knights. The Norman court that inspired so many of the details of the romance can most easily be summoned up in the church of **St Materiana** perched on the clifftop a short distance away, with its altars, candles, round arches and tiny windows.

Other sights in the village of Tintagel itself include **King Arthur's Great Halls**, an extraordinary building constructed out of solid granite in 1933 by Masonic-style enthusiasts, with some exceptional stained-glass windows, and the **Old Post Office** ① *(NT), T01840-770024, www.nationaltrust.org.uk, late Mar-Oct daily 1100-1730 (-1600 in Oct, Nov), £3.60, under-17s £1.80, family £9*, a wonderfully weathered stone cottage dating from the 14th century, with one of its rooms restored to its role as a Victorian post office.

A mile or so south of Tintagel, the beautiful beach at **Trebarwith Strand** (sandy only at low tide) is reached over wonderful stream-gouged rocks and delightful paddling pools, overlooked by a few beach shops, teashops and holiday homes. Lovely walks head up into the woods round about. After 5 miles the coast path south arrives in the little fishing village of **Port Isaac**, renowned for its crab and lobster catch but worth avoiding in high season when visitors clog the narrow streets. Nearby **Port Quin** is similar, but less commercialized. The sad little Gothic tower on **Doyden Point** close by commemorates the loss of the Portquin boat with all hands.

Also very busy in summer, but this time with surfers and their sport, is the seaside resort of **Polzeath** just round the spectacular lonely headland of Pentire Point. From their fine position at the foot of the Pentire peninsula, the holiday homes of Polzeath look down on the wide curve of the bay where cars pull up on the beach in their hundreds much of the year, wet-suited boarders running for the breakers to escape the crowds and join their own. A charming coast path leads round to **Trebetherick**, where the pet poet of Middle England John Betjeman is buried in the graveyard of the old church of St Enodoc, half-buried itself in the sand. **Daymer Bay** here is another good spot for surfing. A mile further, strung along the Camel estuary looking across to Padstow (see page 62), connected by foot ferry, the village of **Rock** has become known as 'Fulham-on-Sea' thanks to the influx of second-homers from London.

Bodmin Moor → *For listings, see pages 65-67.*

Inland, east of Tintagel, the wide tract of bleak granite upland that comprises Bodmin Moor is surrounded by surprisingly beautiful gardens. At **Pencarrow House** ① *Washaway, T01208-841369, www.pencarrow.co.uk Apr-Oct Sun-Thu, £10.50, under-15s £5, family £28*, there are 50 acres of woodland around this little stately home

Cornwall for the Cornish

'After you've rinsed the glus-dyns out of your mouth with dowr, you might feel like taking a tollgar down to the treth through fields full of woolly davas'. Apologies to Mebyon Kernow – the Cornish separatist party – for the attempt at Cornglish, but then they're likely anyway to have more important matters in hand than cleaning their teeth for a taxi ride to the beach through the sheep fields. The Cornish language, closely related to Breton, belongs to the family of Celtic tongues of which Irish Gaelic remains the most robust member. Like Scottish Gallic, it flourished until the 17th century, when a combination of official repression and local snobbery contributed to its decline. Unlike the Gallic, by the late 19th century it had died out completely as a native tongue, although the scholastic efforts around that time of one Henry Jenner ensured its survival. What is now called Standard Cornish was developed in the last century under the guidance of Morton Nance. More information on learning the language and contributing to its revival can be found at www.clas.demon.co.uk.

Meanwhile, Cornish separatists are gaining growing support for their vision of a self-governing county, a backlash against perceived ignorance of the area's economic plight in Westminster. The possibility of a devolved assembly for the region is in fact being discussed, in English.

with a world-renowned parkland of specimen conifers. Formal gardens designed by Sir William Molesworth boast many varieties of rhododendrons and camellias. From the house one views geometric gardens with a fine turf maze, Victorian rockery from Bodmin Moor, palm trees and peacocks fanning their tails. Pencarrow, in its unpretentious grandness, makes for a leisurely and gracious day out.

Much better known, **Lanhydrock** ① (NT), near Bodmin, T01208-265950, www.national trust.org.uk, Mar-Nov Tue-Sun from 1100, garden year round daily from 1000, £11, child £5.45, family £27.50, is a magnificent estate with formal parterres surrounded by yew and box and unusual circular herbaceous borders, designed in 1857, as well as some exceptional magnolias. This is also the grandest house in Cornwall, so a house and gardens visit could make for a lovely afternoon.

Nearby, towards Lostwithiel in the valley of the River Fowey, **Restormel Castle** ① (EH), T01208-872687, www.english-heritage.org.uk, Apr-Sep daily 1000-1800, Oct daily 1000-1700, £3.50, under-16s £2.10, is a remarkable Norman castle, much of its extraordinary circular keep still standing and in very good condition. Once the home of Edward, the Black Prince, its commanding position on a round wooded hillock gives fine views across the countryside around. On Bodmin Moor itself, **Dozmary Pool** is considered to be the most likely spot to find Excalibur and the Lady of the Lake, if you fancy looking. Otherwise, there are moorland walks to be had all around. A little to the south, the church in the little town of **St Neot** is worth travelling to for its magnificent stained glass, telling the story of Adam and Eve.

Padstow and around → *For listings, see pages 65-67.*

Back on the crowded coast, across the Camel Estuary from Rock, Padstow is a busy fishing and holiday harbour town, made famous and apparently almost single-handedly kept in business by celebrity chef Rick Stein. People still travel for miles to eat in one of his several fish restaurants here. Others are happy just to wander around the old streets sloping down to the harbourside or pick up some absolutely fresh shellfish when the boats come in.

The **National Lobster Hatchery** ① *T01841-533877, www.nationallobster hatchery.co.uk, year round daily from 1000, £3.50, under-16s £1.50, family £7.50,* on the quayside opens its doors to visitors interested in the farming and life-cycle of the delicious things with tasty pincers. This quirky quayside attraction at the head of the Camel Trail is good for nippers of both the curly haired and crustacean variety. Lobsters are hatched and reared here before being released into the wild to replenish stocks around Cornwall. You can peer through portholes into the high-tech laboratory where planktonic lobster larvae swirl about inside giant glass cylinders, and tiny juveniles squat in ice-cube size containers. It takes up to seven years for them to reach maturity - if given the chance, lobsters can live for 100 years and grow to nearly 2 m in length! Dai the Claw is already halfway there. He's one of the hatchery's resident lobsters, inhabiting a small display of immaculate tanks, along with Charlie the albino lobster, Thermidor the orange-coloured lobster (a one-in-10-million occurrence), Sennen the spider crab, Gordon the edible crab and a trio of sponge crabs called Sponge Bob, Sponge Bill and Sponge Bert. Crustaceans have never seemed so cuddly and your children may never want to eat seafood again (parents, meanwhile, will be drooling over the recipe suggestion - grilled lobster with pernod and olive oil dressing - that's been sneaked into the display). Don't miss the rock-pool tank where domed glass provides a magnified view of blennies, crabs and anemones. There's also a small craft table with puzzles and colouring sheets, some fun interpretation boards about lobster life cycles and marine conservation, plus a chance to adopt a lobster.

Named after St Petrock, who came over from Ireland in a coracle, Padstow provided sanctuary for criminals before the Reformation and was once packed with shrines to saviour saints. **St Petrock's**, the town church on the hill, is the only one to survive, its 15th-century tower resting on a 13th-century base.

Just outside Padstow, **Prideaux Place** ① *near Padstow, T01841-532411, www.prideaux place.co.uk, Easter-Oct Sun-Thu from 1230, £6, under-16s £3,* is a small Elizabethan house in a superb position overlooking the estuary. Modified in the 18th century, with attractive gardens, it's been in the hands of the same family for the last 400 years and has become a popular film location. It's also where Humphrey Prideaux, Dean of Norwich in 1702, wrote a Life of Mahomet. At **Trevone Bay**, near St Cadoc's Point, the shoreline is full of intriguing rock pools with a rare population of sea slugs.

Newquay and around → *For listings, see pages 65-67.*

South along the coast road from Padstow, the 3-mile stretch of sand at Watergate Bay hosts Jamie Oliver's Fifteen restaurant and is a good place to learn to surf and introduces the capital of surf culture in the UK at Newquay. Although it does have a

The Camel Trail

Cornwall's most popular cycling adventure, the 18-mile Camel Trail, links Padstow, Wadebridge, Bodmin and Wenfordbridge via a largely traffic-free route that follows an old railway track alongside the River Camel.

The trail is divided into three main sections: Padstow to Wadebridge, five miles, flat all the way; Wadebridge to Bodmin, six miles, with a small climb to Bodmin; and, finally, the slightly more challenging seven-mile sector between Bodmin and Wenfordbridge. You could also try a circular route to Rock and catch the ferry back to Padstow.

Allow 45 minutes each way for the estuary-side pedal between Padstow and Wadebridge. You can hire bikes at either town. This often busy section (used by walkers and birdwatchers as well as cyclists) follows the south bank of the estuary, crossing the old iron bridge over Little Petherick Creek and ducking under the A39 bypass before reaching Wadebridge. Stop en route for a picnic or encourage tired legs with the promise of Granny Wobbly's fudge in Wadebridge or ice-cream at Stein's Deli if you're Padstow-bound.

Intrepid cyclists can push on past Wadebridge to Bodmin, where the Camel Trail delves into beautiful riverside woodland. For refreshments, stop at the Camel Valley Vineyard or Camel Trail Tea Gardens near Nanstallon or make for the picnic tables at Grogley Halt, where there's access to the river. Look out for a steam train at Boscarne Junction, the western terminus of the Bodmin and Wenford Railway.

From Dunmere (near Bodmin), the Camel Trail loops north towards Poley's Bridge and Wenfordbridge. This is the quietest section of the trail, climbing gently through beech woodland with views of the river below. There is a seasonal tea room at Tresarrett, while the Blisland Inn makes a worthwhile one-mile detour off the trail.

tiny harbour, Newquay has been pretty much taken over by the sport and its enthusiasts and has the biggest and busiest beaches in Cornwall. Once a fairly quiet family holiday resort, it now imitates Ibiza-style nightlife, can easily be reached on low-cost flights, and milks youth culture for all its worth. **Watergate and Fistral Bays** are the most popular beaches for the sport, at either end of the scale in difficulty, Fistral particularly unpredictable in the challenges it throws up. The **Extreme Academy** on Watergate Bay has won a reputation for reliable instruction in way-out ways to enjoy the beaches, from kite-surfing to stand-up paddleboarding to land-yachting. Most of the locals only return or come out of their houses in winter, while a huge number of B&Bs and guesthouses compete ever more fiercely for the passing trade throughout the year. Best of the beaches is **Lusty Glaze**, a naturally sheltered privately run cove, with exceptionally high water quality and headquarters of the National Lifeguard Training Centre.

Five miles inland, the proud Victorian town of **St Columb Major** could hardly be more different. Much less affected by the tourist industry, the grand buildings of this hilltop town have remained largely unspoiled, clustered around a 15th-century church overlooking the wonderfully green Vale of Mawgan. One oddity near here is the **Japanese Garden and Bonsai Nursery** ⓘ *T01637-860116, www.thebonsainursery.com,* *year round daily 1000-1800, £4.50, child £2,* in St Mawgan Village, based on an actual Zen garden, it's an acre and a half of Japanese maples, azaleas, abundant grasses, bamboo and a 'teahouse', with a Bonzai nursery next door.

A couple of miles to the west of St Columb Major, **Castle-an-Dinas** is a great Iron Age hill fort, while the **Nine Maidens**, also worth a visit, are an ancient stone avenue beneath a wind farm on the Breock Downs to the northwest. **Trerice** ① *(NT), Kestle Mill, Newquay, T01637-875404, £7.20, child £3.60, family £18, house and gardens,* is a very popular gem of an Elizabethan house and garden with a fruit orchard. Its gold and purple colour scheme bursts into full bloom in the summer.

North Cornish Coast listings

For hotel and restaurant price codes and other relevant information, see pages 9-13.

🛏 Where to stay

Bude and Boscastle p58
££££-£££ Wooldown Farm Cottages, Marhamchurch, Bude, T01288-361216, www.wooldown.co.uk. Luxury self-catering cottages sleeping up to 8, with spa baths and 4-poster beds.

££ Trevigue, Crackington Haven, near Bude, T01840-230492, www.trevigue.co.uk. The Crocker family farm has small plots of worked land produce, eggs from heaven, and their own bacon and sausages. The stone house is a stone's throw from the sea. Period features surrounded by a cobbled courtyard and lush verdant foliage.

Tintagel and around p59
£££ Longcross Hotel, Port Isaac, T01208-880243, www.longcrosshotel.co.uk. Perched high above Port Quin with 4 acres of gardens and superb views along the coast.

£££ The Mill House Inn Trebarwith Strand, Nr Tintagel, T01840-770200, www.themillhouseinn.co.uk. Stone building with 8 double en suite rooms that are understated but luxurious. The old mill is surrounded by fully mature pines. Excellent gastropub serving fine seafood, real ales and good wine selection.

££ Cornish Tipi Holidays, Tregeare, Pendoggett, St Kew, T01208-880781, www.cornishtipiholidays.co.uk. Spacious and surprisingly comfortable wigwags with authentic Native American designs, woodland and spring-fed quarry lake for boating and fishing.

Bodmin Moor p60
£££ Anchorage House, Nettles Corner, Tregehan, T01726-81407, www.anchorage house.co.uk. This Georgian house has been meticulously cared for and won awards for its B&B accommodation, facilities and meals. Dinners cost £20 per person. There is even a 15-m-long lap pool and a small gym.

£££-££ Cabilla Manor, near Mount, Bodmin, T01208-821224, www.cabilla.co.uk. An 18th-century manor with tennis court and manicured lawns. Stroll in the gardens and over the edge into Bodmin Moor.

£££-££ Porteath Barn, St Minver, near Wadebridge, T01208-863605. Restored 19th-century stone barn with exposed beams and granite walls. The feel is not unlike a Provençal French mas. Fresh flowers and antiques in a chic and cool setting.

££ Bokiddick Farm, Bokiddick, near Lanivet, T01208-831481, www.bokiddickfarm.co.uk. An 18th-century farmhouse on a 200-acre working dairy farm, the breakfasts here are fresh and delicious. Plenty of space to read and take long unobstructed walks in nature.

Padstow and around p62
Padstow Cottage Company, T01841-532633, www.padstowcottage company.co.uk. Portfolio of 35 self-catering cottages in and around the town and the harbour.

Camping
Dennis Cove Camping T01841-532349, www.denniscovecampsite.co.uk. Small sheltered campsite overlooking the estuary and close to the start of the Camel Trail; see box, page 63.

Newquay p62
No one in their right mind would come to Newquay without a surf board and a strong desire to drink copious amounts of alcohol. Consequently, much of the accommodation is of the hostel variety, or surf lodges as they're called here.

££-£ Base Surf Lodge, Tower Rd,
T07766-132124, www.basesurflodge.com.
Overlooking Fistral Beach, with an in-house
surf school.

£ Newquay Surf Lodge, 18 Springfield Rd,
T01637-859700, www.newquaysurf
lodge.co.uk. Original Newquay surf lodge,
close to surf central, Fistral Beach, and the
town centre. There's a lounge area with a
pool table and garden barbeques. Free Wi-Fi
and parking.

Restaurants

Padstow p62
££££ The Seafood Restaurant, Riverside,
T01841-532700, www.rickstein.com. Top of
the range, Rick Stein's restaurant with rooms,
overlooks the estuary and harbour from a
converted granary.

££ Margot's, 11 Duke St, T01841-533441,
www.margotsbistro.co.uk. Another superior
option with good seafood dishes.

££ The Old Custom House,
South Quay, T01841-532359,
oldcustomhousepadstow.co.uk.
Also right on the harbour, and with an
estimable fish restaurant.

££ Rick Stein's Café, 10 Middle St, T01841-
532359, www.rickstein.com. The youthful,
economy version of Mr Stein's fêted seafood
restaurant (see above).

££ Stein's Fish & Chips, South Quay ,
www.rickstein.com. You can eat in or take
away at **Stein's**, but be prepared to queue. It
is pricier than your average chippie but is it
worth it? Portions are a bit measly, but the
flavour really does set it apart. The batter is
thin and doesn't hit your stomach like a
depth charge; the fish is fresh and moist,
and the chips, of course, are proper spuds
and not too soggy. Other seafood on offer
includes hake, monkfish, tiger prawns
and scallops.

Pubs, bars and clubs

Newquay p62
Recommended local club action includes **Tall
Trees**, Tolcarne Rd, T01637-850313,
www.talltreesclub.com. Open until 0200.

What to do

Padstow p62
Boat trips
Jubilee Queen, T07836-798457,
www.padstowboattrips.com. Visits offshore
islands and heads upriver to Wadebridge,
check harbour boards for sailing times.
Padstow Sealife Safaris, T01841-521613,
www.padstowsealifesafaris.co.uk. 2 hr tours
in search of seals, dolphins, basking sharks
and other coastal wildlife.

Cycling
Padstow Cycle Hire, South Quay, Padstow,
T01841-533533, wwwpadstowcyclehire.com.
Bike hire for 18-mile Camel Trail, linking
Padstow, Wadebridge, Bodmin and
Wenfordbridge via a largely traffic-free route
that follows an old railay track alongside the
River Camel. See box, page 63.

Newquay p62
Boat trips
Newquay boat trips, T01637-878886,
www.newquay-harbour.com. 1 or 2 hr cruises
spotting wildlife or mackerel fishing.

Cycling
The Bike Barn, Elm Farm Cycle Centre,
Cambrose, Portreath, T01209-891498,
www.cornwallcycletrails.com. Main cycle hire
centre for Coast to Coast Trail and Mineral
Tramways route.

Surfing
Surfing Great Britain, surfinggb.com.
See their website for a list of surf schools in
the area.

Extreme Academy, Watergate Bay, Newquay, T01637-860543, www.watergatebay.co.uk. Offer surf lessons and introductory courses in kitesurfing, surf kayaking and stand-up paddleboarding.

⊖ Transport

Newquay *p62*
Taxi
A2B taxis, T01637-875555, www.newquaytravel.co.uk.

Bluebird Taxis, 8 Station Parade, T01637-852222, www.newquay-airport-taxis-direct.co.uk.

ⓘ Directory

Newquay *p62*
Hospitals Newquay Hospital, St Thomas Rd, T01637-893600.

South Cornish Coast

The big noise in South Cornwall since the end of the 20th century has been the Eden Project, near St Austell. This astonishing conversion of a disused clay pit still causes controversy in the local area, but visitors to its two enormous 'biomes' are generally not disappointed (once they manage to get in) by the stunning array of international plantlife inside and the Project's upbeat, colourful and urgent ecological message. Sailing perilously close to becoming a victim of its own success, it's not the only attraction that this part of the county has to offer, although gorgeous gardens are something of a theme. Just across the water from Plymouth, Rame Head is the isolated and scenic coastal setting for Mount Edgcumbe's formal gardens and country park, near the lonely mariner's chapel of St Michael. To the north, the Tamar Valley is a wooded riverside wonderland.

Back on the coast, Fowey is a still fairly unspoiled harbour fishing town, a fate that others like Looe, Mevagissey and Polperro have not managed to avoid. Beyond St Austell, the coast to St Mawes hides tiny harbours like charming Portloe. Falmouth's naval legacy and lively contemporary art scene are worth lingering around for, while outside the towns and villages, the natural beauty of the area is as stunning as it is varied.

The Lizard peninsula stretches 12 miles south from Helston and the secluded charms of the Helford Estuary to the spectacular crags and crashing waves of Britain's most southerly point. Delightful subtropical gardens, secluded fishing villages, rocky coves and miles of unspoilt coastal paths draw in considerable crowds around the summer. The mild climate also keeps The Lizard warm in winter, and off-season primroses may be found here before Christmas and even daffodils in January.

Visiting the South Cornish Coast

Getting there

From Plymouth the lovely Tamar Valley line runs up to Gunnislake. Regular buses link Bodmin Parkway, a beautiful station on the main London to Penzance line, with Padstow. Falmouth is on a branch line 20 minutes from Truro, trains run every 1 hour 30 minutes or so. Change at Truro for mainline services to Penzance in the west or Exeter (2 hours) and London (7-8 hours) in the east. **National Rail Enquiries**, T08457-484950, www.nationalrail.co.uk.

From Plymouth the A38 runs up to Liskeard, from where the A390 forks off to St Austell. Plymouth to the Eden Project should take about 45 minutes. National Express, T08717-818178, www.nationalexpress.com, run regular coaches from London Victoria to St Austell (7 hours). The A39 takes you 20 minutes southwest to Falmouth from Truro traffic depending (double road journey times in high season) and the A393 will bring you over from the north coast via Redruth in about the same time. Helston is about 30 minutes southwest on A394. The A3083 takes you 40 minutes south, down the spine of the peninsula to the Lizard Point, with smaller roads to Mullion on the west and St Keverne and Coverack in the east.

National Express run numerous buses from Falmouth to destinations including twice daily to London, (7½ hours), Bristol (6 hours), and twice daily to Penzance (1 hour).

Five of the best beaches in Cornwall

· **Strangles** for rock formations, seclusion and naturists, page 59.
· **Daymer Bay** for very good windsurfing, page 60.
· **Lusty Glaze** is very safe and clean for swimmers, page 63.
· **Whitesands Beach** at Sennen Cove is one of Cornwall's best surf beaches, page 79.
· **St Martin's Flats**, Isles of Scilly, for wildlife and seclusion, page 89.

Getting around

Cars overload the area in summer so go on **foot** or **bicycle** wherever you can. The Clay Trails cycle route, T0845-113 0065, www.sustrans.org.uk, links Bugle with the Eden Project along 4 miles of level track. Scenic bus services operated by First, T0845-600 1420, www.firstgroup.com, include the No 35 (Falmouth to Helston, via Helford Passage and Gweek) and the No 81B (Plymouth to Polperro, via East Looe). A network of ferries, boats, buses and trains, **Fal River Links**, www.falriver.co.uk, link Falmouth, Truro, St Mawes and the Roseland.

Tourist information

Falmouth TIC ① *11 Market Strand, T01326-312300, www.acornishriver.co.uk.* **Fowey** ① *South St, T01726-833616, www.fowey.co.uk.* **Helston** TIC ① *Meneage St, T01326-565431.* **Launceston** ① *Market House Arcade, Market St, T01566-772321, www.visitlaunceston.co.uk.* **Liskeard** ① *Forester's Hall, Pike St, T01579-349148, www.liskeard.gov.uk.* **Looe** TIC ① *The Guildhall, Fore St, T01503-262072.* Mevagissey i *St Georges Sq, T01726-844857.* **St Austell** TIC ① *Southbourne Rd, T01726-879500, www.visit thecornishriviera.co.uk.* **St Mawes** TIC ① *Roseland Visitor Centre, The Square, T01326-270440, www.roselandinfo.com.* **Tamar Valley Tourism Association** ① *6 Fore St, Calstock, T01822-835874, www.tamarvalley tourism.co.uk.* **Truro** ① *Boscawen St, T01872-274555, www.truro.gov.uk.*

East Cornwall → *For listings, see pages 74-76.*

Rame

The most easterly part of Cornwall, **Rame Head** is still distinctively Cornish. Much of it is taken up with the grounds of **Mount Edgcumbe House and Country Park** ① *Cremyll, Torpoint, T01752-822236, www.mountedgcumbe.gov.uk, Apr-Sep Sun-Thu 1100-1630, £7.20, concessions £5.50, under-16s £3.25, family £16*, now owned by Plymouth City Council. The Cremyll Ferry from Admiral's Hard, in the Stonehouse district of Plymouth, provides the best approach to the house itself, the first country house in England to be built for its prospect. Badly bombed in the Second World War, the interior is now less full of treasures than it might have been, but the gardens still command great views of Plymouth Sound. The formal gardens, near the Cremyll Ferry landing, are also special, laid out in the 18th century and divided into French, Italian, English, and more recently American and New Zealand styles. The Earl's Garden, behind the house, was laid out at the same time, and features magnificent cedars, classical garden houses and a shell seat. Two miles away is the small village of Rame, with its candlelit old church, while right out on the headland, 20 minutes' walk from the village, is the lonely St Michael's mariners chapel, with coastguards' cottages and radio mast for company and superb views south, east and west.

Tamar Valley

North of Plymouth, Cornwall's border with Devon runs up the picturesque Tamar Valley, passing close to Tavistock, on the edge of Dartmoor, and up beyond Launceston. Trains run the 14 miles from Plymouth to Gunnislake via Bere Ferrers, Bere Alston and Calstock on the scenic **Tamar Valley Line** throughout the year, crossing the Tavy and Tamar on a series of great viaducts. **Boat cruises** (*Plymouth Boat Trips*, T01752-253153, www.plymouthhoecruises.co.uk) also head upriver to **Calstock**, the unofficial capital of the region, described by John Betjeman as the "least known and most uninterruptedly Cornish town". Just downstream is the estate of **Cotehele** ① (NT), T01579-351346, *www.nationaltrust.org.uk, Apr-Oct Sat-Thu 1100-1700 (-1630 in Oct), garden open all year daily 1030-dusk (last admission 30 mins before closing), £9, child £4.50, family £22.50, garden and mill only £5.40/£2.70/£13.50*, the ancient seat of the Edgcumbe family. A wonderful medieval house built between 1485 and 1627, without electric light, it's surrounded by beautiful woodland, as well as being close to a restored watermill, and the old Quay on the river is home to a discovery centre with scale models recreating the scene in the 19th century of coal, limestone and market produce being loaded onto barges for transport down the Tamar River. One of them, the *Shamrock*, is moored outside. A walk through the woods leads to a 15th-century chapel on a bluff overlooking the river, built by Sir Richard Edgcumbe in gratitude for his dramatic escape from Richard III's men, putting his pursuers off the scent by throwing his hat and a big rock into the river.

Looe to Fowey → For listings, see pages 74-76.

Back on the coast, Looe is a typically touristy south Cornish seaside town, still with a few boats working out of its harbour. A walk west round Hannafore Point, though, arrives at a naturalist's dream: a series of gullies and tidepools with an abundant variety of sea flora. Since 1964, the seaside woods around Looe have been set aside for a colony of **woolly monkeys** ① *Monkey Sanctuary, Murrayton, Looe, T01503-262532, www.monkey sanctuary.org, Easter-Sep Sat-Thu 1100-1630, £8, child £5, family £25*, endangered in their natural habitat, the Brazilian rainforest. See them swing through high beech trees, apparently enjoying life in south Cornwall.

Round the corner and Talland Bay, the quaint appeal of the old fishing village of **Polperro** draws thousands to its single valley street of tacky souvenir shops. That said, the old harbour is undeniably picturesque, immortalized by the artist Oskar Kokoshka and despite being a shadow of its former role as a storm-battered fishing boat haven, the village does well as a happy holiday spot in the summer.

Next stop along the coast, **Fowey** is a dear little harbour town, closely associated with the novelist Daphne du Maurier. A deep-water working port, it is also popular with tourists, who drop into the **Du Maurier Literary Centre** in narrow Fore Street running parallel with the waterfront. **St Fimbarrus Church** is also worth a look, as are the town's secret gardens, such as the **Old Boys Grammar School**, alive with roses in summer. Alternatively, climb the granite steps of Bull Hill, or find the small sheltered beach at Cove.

The **Hallwalk** is a memorable 2-mile circular walk with wonderful views across the river to Fowey and down the estuary mouth to Polruan. Catch the ferry across to **Bodinnick**, where there's a wide choice of places to eat. The walk continues to **St Catherine's Point** and the ruins of **St Catherine's Castle**, built by Henry VIII, guarding the entrance to the harbour. Across the river the boat building centre of **Polruan**, with its narrow streets clinging to the hillside leading down to the old waterfront and quay, is less touristy than Fowey and well worth the foot ferry trip.

St Austell to St Mawes → *For listings, see pages 74-76.*

Tregehan
ⓘ *T01726-814389, mid-Mar to late May Wed-Fri, Sun and bank holiday Mon 1030-1700, Jun-late Aug Wed 1300-1630, £6, under-16s free, http://tregrehan.org.*
This is an old-fashioned garden in the area which is worth seeking out. At Par, near St Austell, Tregehan has an imposing 1846 glasshouse (making a useful comparison with the Eden Project's biomes) and a formal walled garden. These 20 delightful acres have belonged to the Carlyon family since since 1565. There are lovely terraces and colourful border scheme, as well as a focus on genera from temperate regions and a green gene bank for source plants. The camellias are award winning. Stroll down a path of yews to a doggie graveyard and statues of beloved and lost dogs. Fully mature oaks shelter them in the parkland. There is also a nursery here and cottages to rent.

Eden Project
ⓘ *Bodelva, T01726-811911, www.edenproject.com. Year round daily from 1000 (car parks open 0900 during summer school holidays), £23, concessions £18.50, under-16s £10.50, under-4s free (discounts available if you walk, cycle or take public transport, Jungle Cycle Hire, Bugle, T01726-852204).*
North of St Austell is the main event in south Cornwall, sometimes with queues 10 miles away from the site, and signs saying 'Eden Full'. The Eden Project is not a wet weather attraction apparently, but no one's listening. Then again, it has gathered very positive worldwide publicity. Architecturally stunning, educationally stimulating, and culturally on the money, the Eden Project is an extraordinary enterprise: a 'Living Theatre of Plants and People' as it likes to bill itself, its highlights are the great high-tech greenhouses in an abandoned chinaclay pit: the **Rainforest Biome** for jungle plantlife is the largest and most spectacular. Slightly smaller, the **Mediterranean Biome** contains thousands of plants from South Africa and California. The **Core** educational centre has plenty of interactive exhibits, including an elaborate nut-cracking machine. Seasonal events include summer den-making for children, ice skating, Christmas markets and music concerts. Allow at least three hours to see the whole thing.

Coastal villages
The coast from St Austell to St Mawes has remained remarkably unspoiled, partly because it's more difficult to reach by road. At **Mevagissey**, a crowed little fishing village in summer, roads of any size peter out, leaving the rest of the coast relatively quiet. Inland, **Caerhays Castle Garden** ⓘ *Porthluney Cove, T01872-501310, www.caerhays.co.uk, £7.50 garden, £7.50 house, £12.50 combined,* was created by JC Williams' sponsored plant

gathering expeditions to China in the 19th century. The bounty of his efforts are visible today with rare shrubs and flowers delighting the eye in a wooded garden. Noteworthy are the camellias again, magnolias and rhododendrons. On rolling hills the castle estate offers tea with walks winding down to the sea.

More well-known perhaps are the **Lost Gardens of Heligan** ① *Pentewan, T01726-845100, www.heligan.com, Apr-Sep, daily 1000-1800, Oct-Mar daily 1000-1700, £10, under-16s £6, family £27,* with over 80 acres making it apparently the largest restored garden in Europe. Miles of footpaths have been uncovered and reinstated with thousands of newly planted trees providing shelter. There are walled gardens with exotic plants, a melon house, Italian garden, woodland walks weaving past statues, boardwalks threading through a jungle of bamboos and tree ferns, a wildlife hide with CCTV footage of bats, birds and badgers, a superb farm shop and a tea room serving soups, snacks and roast lunches.

A series of tiny villages are sprinkled along the rocky coast. **Portloe** is one of the most attractive, with its minuscule landing slip, cliffwalks and jolly tearooms. Further west, dinky little **St Mawes** looks across to Falmouth across Carrick Roads. **Lamorran House Gardens** ① *T01326-270800, www.lamorrangarden.co.uk, Apr-Sep, £7.50, under-16s free,* is a beautiful 4-acre tropical garden with a Mediterranean grace and gorgeous views to St Antony's Headland and the sea. As with other gardens in Cornwall the mild climate allows the most delicate plants to thrive: azaleas, desert agaves and yuccas are just a few examples. Walk amidst statuary and columns and palms set in a landscape inspired by an Englishman's garden abroad.

Falmouth → *For listings, see pages 74-76.*

Though one of Cornwall's largest towns, Falmouth is perhaps the least dominated by tourists. There is a large art student community and the world's second deepest natural harbour has so far dissuaded the Navy from embarking. Seeded on the slopes of three buxom hillocks, Falmouth grew from the inconsequential hamlets of Smithwick and Arwenack to a bustling town at the centre of the Old World's postal system. There are three excellent **beaches** within easy reach – Gyllyngvase, Swanpool and Maenporth. The outstanding **National Maritime Museum** ① *T01326-313388, www.nmmc.co.uk, year round daily 1000-1700, £10.50, under-15s £7.20, under-5s free, family £29.50,* has an impressive collection of boats old and new as well as themed exhibitions on everything from survival at sea to Cornish maritime heritage. The Look Out offers panoramic views over Falmouth harbour, while the Tidal Zone provides a window on its marine life. **Pendennis Castle** ① *T01326-316594, www.english-heritage.org.uk, year round daily from 1000, £6.50, concessions £5.90, child £3.90, family £16.90,* is Cornwall's oldest and offers splendid views though never had quite the range that Henry VIII was looking for: it was still possible to sail up the river out of range of both Pendennis and St Mawes opposite. **Falmouth Art Gallery** ① *T01326-313863, www.falmouthartgallery.com, Mon-Sat 1000-1700,* has an interesting collection and is popular with (and even encourages) families.

Neighbouring **Penryn** is a quiet little town that also happens to be among the oldest in the country. It was the site of Glasney College – a centre of learning and pilgrimage until the Reformation – and there is little doubt that the town would have claimed Truro's cathedral had Henry VIII and successive generations of builders left it standing. Not that there was much need for scavenging as Penryn remains at the centre of some of the best granite quarries in the world.

Helston → *For listings, see pages 74-76.*

While the town has a noble history, gentrification started early and a magnificent bowling green dating from 1764 now stands on the site of the castle built by Edward The Confessor's brother. At the entrance to the green stands an impressive Victorian Gothic arch, commemorating the hero of a battle against the closure of a local mine, but unless you've timed your visit to coincide with the celebration of **Furry Dance** on St Michael's Day, you'll find it is the monuments to late 20th century tourism that dominate the rest of the town. A **Folk Museum** ① *T01326-564027, 1000-1700 all year,* is housed in the old Market House and details the social and industrial history of the Lizard peninsula.

Lizard Peninsula → *For listings, see pages 74-76.*

The **Helford Estuary** would quell arguments even on the most demanding of family holidays. Nature lovers are particularly spoiled with the **National Seal Sanctuary** ① *T01326-221361, www.sealsanctuary.co.uk, daily from 1000, £13, child £10, family £36* a rehabilitation centre for common and grey seals rescued around Cornwall's coast, with lovely creekside walks to enclosures containing more exotic creatures such as sea lions, fur seals and Asian short-clawed otters. With its 150-year-old laurel maze, **Glendurgan** ① *(NT), T01326-250906, www.nationaltrust.org.uk, Tue-Sat, Feb-Oct 1030-1730, £6.80, child £3.50 family £17.10,* at the eastern end of the river, is one of the great subtropical gardens of the Southwest. Exotic trees and shrubs flourish amidst open glades carpeted with wild flowers in season. **Trebah Gardens** ① *T01326-250448, www.trebah-garden.co.uk, daily from 1000, £4.40, under-15s £1* has colourful displays of azaleas and rhododendrons in spring and hydrangeas later in the year, the ravine garden ending at Polgwidden Cove where US troops embarked for the D-Day landings at Omaha Beach in Normandy. **Trevarno** ① *T01326-574274, www.trevarno.co.uk, daily 1030-1700 daily,* brings the green-fingered tally to three.

In the west, follow the coastal path south through rocky **Porthkerris** to warm-hearted **St Keverne** a mile inland. **Coverack**, once a notorious smuggling haunt, retains its charm as a fishing village as does **Cadgwith** with its thatched cottages spilling down into the sea. For a day at the beach, head to the expanse of **Kennack Sands** or the stunning low-tide perfection of **Kynance Cove** on the east coast. The **Lizard** village itself is expanding rapidly preferring quantity to quality but the coves at **Housel Bay** and **Mullion** retain their charm.

The **Lizard Lighthouse Heritage Centre** ① *Lizard Point, T01326-290202, www.lizard lighthouse.co.uk, call for opening times, £6, child £3,* has interactive exhibits to help you navigate the turbulent history of Britain's southernmost lighthouse. If it's size you're after, **Goonhilly** ① *T0800-679593, www.goonhilly.bt.com,* is the largest satellite station in the world, but is currently closed to the public until further notice. Naval and helicopter enthusiasts can call **RNAS Culdrose** ① *T01326-565085,* to arrange a guided coach tour.

South Cornish Coast listings

For hotel and restaurant price codes and other relevant information, see pages 9-13.

🛏 Where to stay

Rame *p69*

The Old Rectory, St John-in-Cornwall, near Torpoint, T01752-822275. Oh so peaceful historic house with many original features, set in lovely wooded grounds with a large pond. Snooker in the afternoon and long views from the bedrooms. Available as a self-catering property through cottages4you.co.uk. It sleeps 10 and costs £2,200 for a week in high season.

Tamar Valley *p70*

£££-££ Botelet, Herodsfoot, Liskeard, T01503-220225, www.botelet.com. Pretty drive and country setting with a choice of organic farmhouse B&B, self-catering cottages, yurts or meadow camping.

££ Mill Cottage, run by the National Trust, T0844-800 2070, www.nationaltrust cottages.co.uk. In the wooded Tamar Valley, this house was built in the 1860s for the miller at Cotehele.

Looe to Fowey *p70*

££££-£££ The Cormorant Hotel, Golant, near Fowey, T01726-833426, www.cormoranthotel.co.uk. On a hillside with a spellbinding view of the River Fowey, this is truly an enchanted part of Britain. This hotel is well managed with many amenities, including an award-winning two-rosetted restaurant (**££**). Glorious views from most rooms. There's a heated pool and you can use it as a base for numerous walks into the countryside.

St Austell to St Mawes *p71*

££££-£££ The Lugger, Portloe, Truro, T01872-501322, www.luggerhotel.co.uk. Perched atop the tiny harbour, this

22-bedroom hotel is a treasure. Let the staff know if lobster is your thing and the local fishermen will bring it in. People travel for this restaurant (**££**). Meticulously clean and fresh. A small and romantic hotel.

£££ Creed House, Creed, Grampound, Truro, T01872-530372, www.creedhouse.co.uk. This listed house with outstanding gardens is notable for its gracious hospitality.

£££ Nanscawen Manor House, Prideaux Rd, Luxulyan Valley, Par, T01726-814488, www.nanscawen.com. Set in the heart of a woodland this 16th-century manor house has an abundance of charm. Lovely light in the 4 luxury suites and panoramic views.

££ Crugsillick Manor, run by Classic Cottages, T01326-555555, www.classic.co.uk. This Queen Anne manor house, comprising 3 self-catering cottages, is a perfect stopover for the pillage and plunder tour of Cornwall. A winding smugglers' path takes you down to the sea from the house. The splendid plaster ceiling was moulded by Napoleonic prisoners which the former owner Admiral Sir Arthur Kemp brought back from seafaring adventures. He apparently still haunts the place.

Falmouth *p72*

£££ Budock Vean Hotel, Falmouth, T01326-250288, www.budockvean.co.uk. Spectacular gardens on the banks of the Helford River, near very fresh crabs at the **Ferryboat Inn**. Indoor pool, spa, 9-hole golf course, tennis courts, fishing, boat trips and 4 luxury self-catering cottages.

Helston *p73*

££££-£££ Nansloe Manor, near Helston, T01326-558400, www.nansloe-manor.co.uk. A Grade II listed building, parts of which date back to the 1600s. Set in 4 acres, the property is further surrounded by woodland and farmland, and has 15 luxurious rooms.

Lizard Peninsula *p73*
£££ The Housel Bay Hotel, at the southernmost tip, T01326-290417, www.houselbay.com. A number of high Victorian hotels dot the area, this is one of the best, with its piano bar, eclectic photograph collection and warm welcome. Although there are countless B&Bs in the area, they do get booked quickly. Try **££-£ Trevinock Guest House**, St Keverne, T01326-280498, www.trevinock.co.uk. Self-catering for longer visits is highly recommended: **Lizard Lighthouse Cottages**, T01326-240333, www.cornishcottages online.com; **Heath Farm Cottages**, T01326-280521, www.heath-farm-holidays.co.uk; **Cadgwith Cove Cottages**, T01326-290764, www.cadgwithcove cottages.co.uk.

Camping
Widely available; try: **Little Trevothan**, Coverack, T01326-280260, www.little trevothan.co.uk; or **Skyburriowe Farm**, Garras, T01326-221646, www.sky burriowefarm.co.uk.

Restaurants

Looe to Fowey *p70*
££ Food for Thought, Fowey, T01726-832221, www.foodfor thought.fowey.com. A small cottage on the harbourside. There are choices for those of you who don't fancy seafood but this is what people have been coming back for, for some 40 years. The **Boathouse** offers a more bistro feel with slightly cheaper pizza and pasta dishes.

St Austell to St Mawes *p71*
££ The Rosevine Hotel, Rosevine, Portscatho, T01872-580206, www.rosevine.co.uk. Enjoy a seafood

platter in the lovely garden that leads down to the cliff's edge, or order a packed lunch from the deli service. It's also a fine Georgian house with 12 apartments and suites.
£ Sharksfin, The Quay, Mevagissey, T01726-842969, www.thesharksfin.co.uk. The Sharksfin is set right on the harbour of this pretty but crowded little fishing village. The restaurant is renowned for fresh seafood, all bought straight from the local fishermen. Lobster, mussels, shellfish, plaice, sea bass are standards on the daily menu.

Falmouth *p72*
££ Best Western Penmere Manor Hotel, T0800-980 4611, www.penmeremanor hotel.co.uk. Splash out with the finest local fish and meat. Accommodation consists of 37 superior en suite rooms with free Wi-Fi (**£££-££**).
££ Indaba Fish on the Beach, Swanpool, T01326-311866, www.indabafish.co.uk. Offers fine seafood in a lovely location.
££ Trengilly Wartha Inn, T01326-340332, trengilly.co.uk. In a lovely setting at Constantine, west of Falmouth, near the Helford River. Bar food at lunchtime, the Full Monty at dinner (book ahead and stay for the night, **££**).

Helston *p73*
Pasties, ice creams and junk food come at you from all sides in Helston. But for more natural produce try the **Farmer's Market** Sat 0830-1300 at Helston's boating lake.
£ Cadgwith Cove Inn, T01326-290513, www.cadgwithcoveinn.com. Delightful but crowded pub serving up home-cooked seafood caught the same day by local fishermen.

Lizard Peninsula *p73*
££ Halzephron Inn, Gunwalloe, T01326-240406, www.halzephron-inn.co.uk. Wonderful westerly views, award-winning meals and a good wine list.

££ The White Hart, St Keverne,
T01326-280325, www.thewhitehart
lizard.co.uk. Traditional inn on the Acorn Trail,
popular with walkers.

◑ Pubs, bars and clubs

Helston *p73*
£ Blue Anchor, 50 Coinagehall St,
T01326-562821, www.spingoales.com.
A 15th-century inn brewing powerful
'Spingo' ales with water from a nearby well.

✪ Entertainment

Falmouth *p72*
Many of the pubs organize theme nights and
karaoke as well as the odd concert. Look out
for details of local entertainments in the local
press and the weekly guide available free
across the area. See falmusic.co.uk for
full listings.
The Star and Garter, Old High St, Falmouth.
Mon jazz nights.

✿ Festivals

Looe to Fowey *p70*
May Fowey Festival. Fowey and the
surrounding area hold this renowned festival
every year, and very popular it is too. There is
also usually free entertainment on
Town Quay.

Falmouth *p72*
Jul-Sep The Tall Ships Race in Jul and a
regatta in Aug while studios open their
doors in Aug- Sep to reveal kitsch coastal
watercolours mingling with some more
interesting contemporary work from the
town's eclectic residents and students from
the art college. Contact **Falmouth Tall Ships
Association**, www.tallshipsfalmouth.co.uk for
details of events

Helston *p73*
May The Furry Dance. 8 May sees Helston's
spring perambulations here. Dancing,
buildings swathed in garlands of flowers,

buskers, stalls and fairground rides take over
the town with much carousing and drinking.

⛰ What to do

Falmouth and Lizard *p72*
Boat trips
Fowey Marine Adventures, Fore St, Fowey,
T01726-832300, www.fowey-marine-
adventures.co.uk, high-speed wildlife cruises.

Horse riding
Bosvathick Riding Stables, Bosvathick
Farm, Constantine, T01326-340367,
www.bosvathickridingstables.co.uk. 92-acre
farm just to the north of the Helford River.
Poltesco Valley Stables, Treal Farm, Ruan
Minor, T01326-240591, www.poltescovalley
stables.com. Beach rides on Kennack Sands.

Walking
The South West Coastal Path is a magnificent
treat for walkers of all levels. Pick up the
invaluable National Trust leaflets at NT car
parks and TICs.

Watersports
Boats are available on the river whatever your
experience: from traditional sailing yawls to
zippy RIBs. Hire is available in Falmouth from
Mylor Boat Hire, T01326-377745,
www.mylorboathire.co.uk, **Loe Beach Boat
Hire**, T01872-864295, www.loebeach.co.uk
and **Helford River Boats**, T01326-250770,
www.helford-river-boats.co.uk. Diving at all
levels can be arranged at T01326-313178,
www.cornishdiving.co.uk or T07816-903260,
www.kennackdiving.co.uk.

⊜ Transport

St Austell to St Mawes *p71*
Bicycle
Pentewan Valley Cycle Hire, West End,
Pentewan, T01726-844242, www.pentewan
valleycyclehire.co.uk. Pedal north on National
Cycle Route 3 to St Austell or south to Lost
Gardens of Heligan and Mevagissey.

Penwith Peninsula

Miles of incomparable coastline offer swathes of golden sand, crystal waters and clifftops strewn with wild flowers, though in less benign mood nature's pounding surf, fierce squalls and treacherous reefs require all the vigilance the area's ubiquitous lighthouses and coastguards can muster. Just as extreme are the contrasts between the impossibly crowded town centres, fit for only the very bravest in high season, and the romantic splendour and unspoilt grandeur of the countryside in between. The delights of exploring a small, well-chosen area on foot keep smitten fans returning year after year. Packing it all in on a whistle stop tour could well ensure a rapid U-turn for the road bound. Where given the opportunity, the taste guardians of the National Trust have achieved the practically impossible, and maintain a delicate balance between the insatiable demands of holidaymakers and the wonderful natural surroundings that draw them. The delights of St Michael's Mount or the coastal path west from St Ives? Or 4D film experience at Land's End? Pay yer money, take yer choice.

Visiting the Penwith Peninsula

Getting there
First Great Western, T08457-000125, www.firstgreatwestern.co.uk, operate trains between London Paddington and Penzance (6 hours), with direct service to St Ives every other hour (5 hours 30 minutes). Penzance is the last major stop on the A30 30 minutes from Redruth, with Land's End another tortuous 9 miles. Turn off 5 miles before Penzance for St Ives and the north coast. The southern coast road takes in Mousehole, Lamorna and Porthcurno on the way to the tip, continuing on through St Just to St Ives. National Express, T08717-818178, www.nationalexpress.com, have several buses a day to London from Penzance (9 hours) or St Ives (8 hours 30 minutes). Local service takes 25 minutes to St Ives every other hour. Newlyn, Mousehole, Land's End, and Zennor are all well served locally but allow plenty of margin at peak times. Traveline, www.travelinesw.com.

Tourist information
Hayle ① *Hayle Library, Commercial Rd, T01736-754399.* **Penzance TIC** ① *Station Approach, T01736-362207, www.visit-westcornwall.com, close by the train and bus stations, 0900-1700 Mon-Fri, 0900-1600 Sat and 1000-1300 Sun.* **St Ives TIC** ① *Guildhall, Street an Pol, T01736-796297, 0900-1700 Mon-Fri, 0900-1600 Sat and 1000-1300 Sun.*

Penzance → *For listings, see pages 82-83.*

Sheltered in the western end of fertile Mount's Bay, this bustling town gets first prize for sticking its head in the sand and getting on with the unglamorous business of being a transport hub. Its shopping streets can hardly be distinguished from any other conventional English town, the seafront does its job as prosaically as possible and the elegant dome perched on the top of the town passes itself off as a Lloyds bank. To be fair though, the 16th and 17th centuries saw the town's embryonic attempts at growth burnt to the ground twice; first by the Spanish and then by the English so perhaps it's no surprise that it prefers to remain inward looking. Hard-working Newlyn is one of the busiest fishing ports in the Southwest. The marina draws a different catch as a drink with the sun setting behind you lighting up the clouds as you look east to The Lizard will keep the shore densely packed even when all the fish are long gone.

Now owned by The Landmark Trust, The **Egyptian House** ① *Chapel St, apartments bookable by the week long in advance (see page 82)*, was built in 1836 by John Lavin, a Penzance mineralogist, to house a geological museum. The former home of a wealthy miller and merchant, **Penlee House** ① *Morrab Rd, T01736-363625, www.penlee house.org.uk, Oct-Apr Mon-Sat 1030-1630, last admission 1600, May-Sep Mon-Sat 1000-1700, last admission 1630, £4.50, under-18s free,* offers a modern gallery concentrating on the Newlyn School of Artists (1880-1930) as well as a fine Natural History and Antiquarian museum covering 6000 years of Cornish history. The **Newlyn Art Gallery** ① *New Rd, T01736-363715, www.newlynartgallery.co.uk, summer Mon-Sat 1000-1700, winter Tue-Sat 1000-1700, free,* displays contemporary work.

St Michael's Mount
① *T01736-710265/710507, www.stmichaelsmount.co.uk, late Mar-Jun Sun-Fri 1030-1730, Jul-Aug Sun-Fri 1030-1730, Sep-early Nov Sun-Fri 1030-1700, last admission 45 mins before castle closes. Most weekends during the season also include admission to the garden, call to check times. £7.50, child £3.75, family £18.75. Boats run regularly at high tide. £1.50 each way, children £1.*

The archangel is said to have appeared in shining form at the top of this spectacular rock, which rises sharply from the sea at the eastern end of Mount's Bay, thereby ensuring that monks, pilgrims, soldiers and aristocrats would conspire to create one of the most picturesque and charming of monuments in the country. A causeway takes you across the sands at low tide, where you may then stroll along the delightful quay before climbing **The Pilgrim's Steps** (not for the infirm or stillettoed) amidst towering pine trees, and cascading subtropical gardens to the castle and chapel of St Michael perched above.

Originally a monastery affiliated with the Benedictines of Mont St Michel in France, it was used as a stronghold and during the Reformation – it was here that the Armada was first sighted – before being converted after the Civil War by the fortunate Col St Aubyn into a family seat of unique distinction. The labyrinth of rooms reflect the Mount's rich history with styles ranging from stark Medieval to playful Rococo. Helpful and welcoming guides are a mine of information while views from the upper levels – whatever the weather – give a powerful yet comforting sensation of being at sea.

Land's End → *For listings, see pages 82-83.*

Nature has been generous to a fault at Land's End, man unfortunately less so. While tourists used to come and enjoy the simple pleasures of taking photos and totting up the miles they'd travelled to get here, the barren splendour of the promontory is now dominated by **Land's End Landmark** ① *T0871-720 0044, www.landsend-landmark.co.uk, Easter-Oct, from 1000, Nov-Easter from 1030, £10, child £7, £25 family all-inclusove, or pay for individual attractions, from £4 adult, £3 child,* with its interactive Arthur's Quest

Barbara Hepworth (1903-1975)

Barbara Hepworth was a key figure in the abstract movement in British art, famous for her 'sculptures with holes'. Her use of this technique grew more complex as she stretched the hole into oval and spiral shapes and, like her friend Henry Moore, created sculptural forms derived from nature, especially inspired by the sea-washed rocks near her home in Cornwall. Born in Wakefield, Yorkshire, Hepworth studied at Leeds School of Art, then from 1921 at the Royal College of Art, before living in Italy for a spell. She met and married the painter Ben Nicholson in 1931 and together they explored the possibilities of abstraction, visiting the studios of Arp, Brancusi, Braque, Picasso and Gabo among others. In 1939, Hepworth moved to St Ives, Cornwall, where she became an influential member of the artistic community, being a founder member of the Penwith Society in 1949. Sadly, in 1975 she died in a fire in her studio in St Ives, where the fine Barbara Hepworth Museum was opened in her memory.

attraction, 4D cinema, air sea rescue motion theatre, Land's End to John o'Groats exhibition, gift shops, cafés and Greeb Farm children's animal park. A short walk will take you on to the coastal path, sweeping north to **Whitesands Beach** in Sennen Cove and south to **Nanjizal**, a secret gem of a cove. Don't look back.

St Ives → *For listings, see pages 82-83.*

The light that drew the eponymous St Ia to embark from her native Ireland on a magic leaf to this beautiful bay 1,500 years ago has inspired artists, writers, surfers and sun worshippers to follow in her footsteps ever since. The town's beaches, cobbled streets and shimmering sea are bathed in a serene brightness that soothes the soul even when the summer season pulls its biggest crowds. The inspirational Tate St Ives, built on the site of an old gasworks, makes as much of a show of the beach and sea through its wide windows and thoughtful design as it does to the illustrious artists the town has inspired. Ben Nicholson, Barbara Hepworth and Bernard Leach are the much celebrated early-20th-century trio while the legacy lives on in the work of Terry Frost and Willy Barnes-Graham. The more discerning visitor may find the numerous smaller galleries and craft shops too commercial but stroll up the steep streets that lead back from the sea front or up to St Nicholas' Chapel and leave the crowds behind, the hidden corners and expansive views flattering you into thinking the many rewarding discoveries on hand your own. A number of good fish restaurants, cafés and colourful pubs cater for the sore-footed and sunburnt but booking in advance for food and accommodation is a must at busier times of the year.

The **Tate St Ives** ① *Porthmeor Beach,T01736-796226, www.tate.org.uk/stives, Mar-Oct daily 1030-1720, Nov-Feb Tue-Sat 1000-1620, £7 or £10 including entry to the Barbara Hepworth Museum (under-18s free),* masterfully complements the inspiring collection of local talent, while temporary exhibitions showcase leading contemporary artists from around the world. To visit the Tate St Ives is to see modern art in a constant state of self-creation, inspiration, artist and viewer all contributing to the whole. An impressive array of work from one of the greatest sculptors of the last century is beautifully arranged at the **Barbara Hepworth Museum** ① *Barnoon Hill, T01736-796226, Mar-Oct daily 1000-1720, Nov-Feb Tue-Sun 1000-1620*, in the house, workshop and garden where she lived from 1949 until 1975. Her bare forms resonate immense power with their calculated simplicity, and are a perfect tonic for overstimulated visitors suffocated by the

St Ives

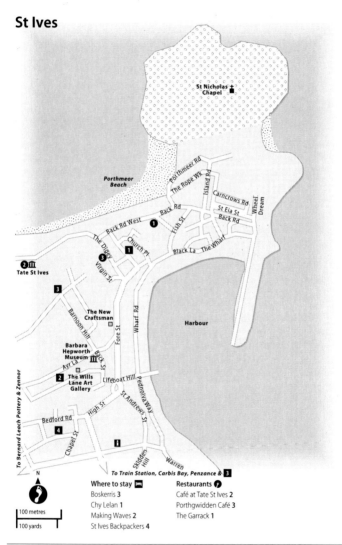

Where to stay 🛏
Boskerris 3
Chy Lelan 1
Making Waves 2
St Ives Backpackers 4

Restaurants 🍴
Café at Tate St Ives 2
Porthgwidden Café 3
The Garrack 1

crowds. The ceramics of Bernard Leach at the **Leach Pottery** ① *Higher Stennack, T01736-799703, www.leachpottery.com, Mar-Oct Mon-Sta 1000-1700, Sun 1100-1600, Nov-Feb Mon-Sat 1000-1700*, inspired by a long stint in Japan, share the same preoccupation with abstraction yet the day to day practicality of his bowls and cups combines function and form with great grace and distinction. Visitors to his pottery will see why he occupies such a pre-eminent and influential position as a ceramicist and will be struck by how contemporary his work appears nearly 100 years later. Other galleries worth seeing in St Ives include the **Wills Lane Art Gallery** and the **New Craftsman**.

Around the Peninsula → *For listings, see pages 82-83.*

The 25-mile stretch of coastline from Penzance to St Ives has some of the most spectacular scenery of the whole **South West Coastal Path** and is well worth exploring. In season, the clifftops are strewn with wild flowers and the mild climate ensures a colourful and botanically diverse display pretty much all year round. The route has it all: sensational coves, towering cliffs, good surf and long clean beaches. Beyond the small but crowded village of Mousehole (pronounced Mowsle), the traffic thins out a little but go by foot and you'll find some space for yourself at any time of the year.

Lamorna Cove and Loggan Rock a few miles further on are beauty spots well worth the name while the beach at **Creen** is charming. If you are in need of intrigue, try the **Porthcurno Telegraph Museum** ① *Porthcurno, T01736-810966, www.porthcurno.org.uk, Apr-Oct daily 1000-1700, Nov-Mar Sun-Mon, 1000-1700, £7.20, child £4.20, family £18*. It was once the largest international cable station and used as a secret communication centre in the Second World War from which contact was kept with Allied forces. **St Just-in-Penwith** is a good base from which to explore the extreme west and the surrounding country is starkly desolate, dotted with prehistoric monuments such as **Lanyon Quoit**, The **Mên-an-Tol** and **Chysauster Iron Age Village**. If you feel like a short stretch of walking, **Zennor to St Ives** is particularly beautiful and can be done in an afternoon or a morning, stoking up a good appetite for lunch and a snooze on the Porthmeor Beach or a well-earned dinner.

Penwith Peninsula listings

For hotel and restaurant price codes and other relevant information, see pages 9-13.

🛏 Where to stay

Penzance *p77*
Self-catering is available at the Egyptian House from **The Landmark Trust**, T01628-825925, www.landmarktrust.org.uk.
£££ The Abbey Hotel, Penzance, T01736-366906, www.theabbeyonline.co.uk. Penzance's finest and worth it if you really do want to stay in town.
£££ The Summer House, T01736-363744, www.summerhouse-cornwall.com. A former artist's home, bright and stylish with good food.
££ Chymorvah, Marazion, T01736-710497, www.chymorvah.co.uk. Overlooking St Michael's Mount, family run and out of the hustle and bustle.

St Ives *p79, map p80*
££££ Tregenna Castle, T01736-795254, www.tregenna-castle.co.uk. 72-acre estate above St Ives, with luxury hotel, self-catering cottages, wooden lodges and abundant leisure facilities.
££££-£££ The Boskerris, in Carbis Bay, T01736-795295, www.boskerrishotel.co.uk. Caters to the comfortable with views out to Godrevy Island.
£££ Chy Lelan, T01736-795844, www.chycor.co.uk/cottages/stives-chylelan . A charming 3 double bedroom fisherman's cottage close to the harbour.
£££ Making Waves, T01736-793895, www.making-waves.co.uk. Luxury self-catering apartments 2 mins from the harbour and beaches.
£ St Ives Backpackers, T01736-799444, www.backpackers.co.uk/st-ives. Basic and informal hostel.

Around the peninsula *p81*
£££ The Gurnard's Head, T01736-796298, www.gurnardshead.co.uk. In a wonderful location high on a cliff top between St Ives and Land's End.
££ Tregurnow Farmhouse, T01736-810255, www.lamorna.biz. A handsome and welcoming farmhouse above Lamorna Cove. Minimum 2-night stay.
££-£ The Old Chapel Backpackers Hostel, Zennor, T01736-798307, www.zennorbackpackers.net. Cheap and peaceful hostel with a good pub to hand and the South West Coastal Path only half a mile away.

🍴 Restaurants

Penzance *p77*
£££ Chapel Street Brasserie & Wine Bar, Chapel St, T01736-350222. Fixed price menu combining Cornish ingredients with French flair.
£££ Mount Haven, Marazion, T01736-710249, www.mounthaven.co.uk. Simple, stylish Cornish cuisine, spectacular views over St Michael's Mount.
££ Bakehouse, Chapel St, T01736-331331, www.bakehouserestaurant.co.uk. Superb food using local ingredients, served in a palm-filled courtyard n the historic part of town.
££ The Hungry Horse, Newlyn, T01736-363446. Has the best of the local fish.
££ The Old Coastguard Hotel, Mousehole, T01736-731222, www.oldcoastguard hotel.co.uk. Superior pub food with more than a hint of fresh seafood, lovely gardens overlooking the sea.
£ The Sail Loft, at the foot of the Mount itself, T01736-710748. Teas and light lunches in National Trust comfort.

Around the peninsula *p81*
£££ The Cornish Range, Mousehole,
T01736-731488, www.cornishrange.co.uk.
Intimate and delightful with rooms upstairs
although quite expensive.
££ The Gurnard's Head, see Where to stay
above. A welcome sight in the wilds of
Zennor with good fish and stunning views.

St Ives *p79, map p80*
££ The Garrack, T01736-796199,
www.garrack.com. Stunning views across the
bay, award-winning contemporary cuisine,
2- or 3-course set menu changes daily.
££ Porthgwidden Café, St Ives,
T01736-796791, www.porthgwidden
cafe.co.uk. Relaxed, friendly café, views
across St Ives Bay, breakfasts, light lunches
and dinners.
££ Porthminster Beach Café,
T01736-795352, www.porthminster
cafe.co.uk. Beachside café serving delicious
local seafood and other dishes for breakfast,
lunch and dinner, using produce from their
very own vegetable plot next door. Prices are
at the higher end of this category.
£ Café at Tate S Ives, T01736-791122,
www.tate.org.uk. Suitably cool yet
unpretentious and has unbeatable views over
the old town and Porthmeor Beach.

Around the Peninsula *p81*
££ Beach, Sennen Cove, T01736-871191,
www.thebeachrestaurant.com. Located
above Whitesand Bay, lunchtime bites,
all-day snack menu, dinner with plenty of
fresh seafood dishes.

🎭 Entertainment

Around the Peninsula *p81*
Acorn Theatre, T01736-363545,
theacornpenzance.com, in an old Wesleyan
Chapel has a lively and varied programme
including dance, comedy, music (especially in
the summer) and drama.
Minack Theatre, T01736-810181, south of
Porthcurno. Outdoor amphitheatre perched
on the cliffside with the best view of any
theatre in the world. Bring something to sit
on, as seats are hard, and a bottle of the best
you can afford and enjoy good performances
of anything from Shakespeare to Alice in
Wonderland. Late May-Sep. Book well
in advance.

🎉 Festivals

Penzance *p77*
21-30 Jun Golowan Festival,
www.golowan.org, fills the town's streets
with processions and music to celebrate
the Feast of St John and the arrival of
midsummer. It culminates in Mazey Day
on the 29th.
Early Aug Morvah Pasty Day.
26 Aug Newlyn Fish Festival,
www.newlynfishfestival.org.uk.
Sep St Ives September Festival,
www.stivesseptemberfestival.co.uk.

🚌 Transport

Penzance *p77*
Car hire Europcar, Albert St, Penzance,
T01736-36881656.

Isles of Scilly

The most southern and westerly outpost of England, the Isles of Scilly are a granite archipelago about 30 miles west-south-west of Land's End. Of around 150 of the low lumps of rock, only five are inhabited, although many more also support vigorous and varied wildlife and flora. The comparatively balmy climate, crystal clear blue water and white sand beaches make this England's best go at a subtropical paradise and a surprisingly good one it is too. Although a very popular family holiday destination in high summer, remarkably the Scilly Isles have not entirely succumbed to the blandishments of year-round mass tourism. After the October half-term school holiday, the Scilly Isles pretty much close down until the next March and get on with growing flowers, fishing and getting online.

The administrative hub of the islands' life is Hugh Town, on St Mary's, the largest of the five although only just over two square miles, but each of the other four main islands have distinctive and independent identities: Tresco is the pretty, glamorous, and exclusive one, with its famous gardens and timeshare cottages; St Martin's sheltered, quieter and hard-working, a naturalist's heaven with amazing beaches; Bryher the most rugged and storm-battered; and self-contained little St Agnes, the furthest south. Boat trips to the uninhabited islands reveal their peculiarities: Samson's deserted village, the Western Rocks for seals (pups in September) and raucous seabird life, Annet for puffins from mid-April to late July, and Bishop's Rock, the most westerly lighthouse in the UK.

Visiting the Isles of Scilly → *For listings, see pages 90-92.*

Getting there

Isles of Scilly Travel, T0845-710 5555, www.ios-travel.co.uk operate Skybus services to the islands, Mon-Sat, from Bristol, Exeter, Land's End, Newquay and Southampton using Twin Otter and Islander aircraft capable of carrying up to 19 people. The . Scillonian III. (book through Isles of Scilly Travel) sails throughout the summer, Monday-Saturday, plus occasional Sunday departures, leaving Penzance at 0915 and arriving at St Mary's around 1200. British International Helicopters used to fly from Penzance Heliport to St Mary's and Tresco, but this service stopped in November 2012.

Getting around

St Mary's Boatmen's Association, T01720-423999, www.scillyboating.co.uk, operate a fleet of 10 passenger ferries linking the islands and offering boat trips to see the area's wildlife and maritime heritage. A noticeboard on the jetty is chalked up with the day's departures. You can buy tickets from the quay kiosk (daily 0930-1015, 1330-1400, later during high season, returns £8.40 adult, £4.20 child) or the TIC (see below).

Tourist information

Hugh Town TIC ① *Hugh St, St Mary's, T01720-424031, www.simplyscilly.co.uk. Easter-Oct Mon-Thu 0830-1730, Fri, Sat 0830-1700, (early Jun-Sep also Sun 1000-1200), Nov-Jan Mon-Fri 0830-1700, Jan-Easter Mon-Fri 0830-1700, Sat 0830-1300.* **St Agnes** ① *Churchtown, T01872-554150.*

Background

Evidence of Bronze Age settlement can be found all over the Isles of Scilly, from a time when they would have formed one solid land mass. In fact there are more burial mounds and chambered cairns on the islands than the rest of Cornwall put together, enough to have given them a reputation in the ancient world for being the Land of the Dead, in the path of the setting sun. The Romans knew the place well, as has been established from finds of Romano-British votive offerings on the now deserted islet of Nornour. Remarkably enough, it's reckoned that the main islands were only separated from each other as recently as the 11th century, giving rise to legends that this flooded valley was where King Arthur lost his life, the lost land of Lyonesse, and also, somehow inevitably, his burial place, Avalon. During the Middle Ages, hermits and heretics colonized the islands, the Benedictine abbey on Tresco being built in 1112, possibly on the site of a Roman temple. Elizabeth I had St Mary's fortified against the Spanish as the great age of sail got underway, and so did the Scilly Isles's notorious reputation for wrecking.

A Royalist stronghold, hotly contested during the Civil War, Charles II took refuge in Star Castle as Prince of Wales for six weeks in 1646 before fleeing to France. Despite the building of the lighthouse on St Agnes in 1680, Sir Cloudesley Shovell and his fleet came to grief on the rocks here in 1707 returning from a raid on Toulon. Only one man survived out of 2000, and Sir Cloudesley himself was slaughtered by an old woman for his emerald ring as he lay gasping on the beach. She confessed on her deathbed, and today a quartz block on St Mary's marks the spot, although the Admiral himself was re-interred in Westminster Abbey.

Neglected and backward through much of the 18th century, the arrival in 1834 of Augustus Smith, who adopted the grand title of Lord Proprietor of the Isles, initiated a controversial reversal in the island's fortunes. Imbeciles were expelled, education made compulsory for all (40 years before the mainland) and the flower industry was born. His descendants still own Tresco, on a long lease from the Duchy, while Hugh Town on St Mary's was only granted freehold in the 1940s.

Increased tourism, thanks in part to Prime Minister Harold Wilson's penchant for holidaying with his dog here in the 60s, has steadily replaced fishing and flower-growing as the islanders' main source of income.

St Mary's

The largest of the islands, a little over two square miles in area, St Mary's is also the most 'normal' of them, although still far from ordinary. Hugh Town, the capital of the archipelago, sits on a sandy isthmus between Town Beach and Porthcressa below the Garrison headland, grey-roofed and whitewashed and unprettified. On Church St, the antiquated local history **museum** ① *T01720-422337, www.iosmuseum.org, Easter- Oct daily 1000-1200, 1330-1630 (also Whitsun-Sep 1930-2100), Nov-Easter Wed 1400-1600, video evenings on Scilly past and present are given on Wed from Jun-Sep at 1945,* tells the story of Scilly with much shipwrecked gear, including a cannon from the wreck of Sir Cloudesley Shovell's *HMS Association* and Roman brooches from Nornour in the Eastern Isles.

The **Garrison Walk** around the headland to the southwest takes about an hour and gives tremendous views of the other islands and an historical insight into the islands' strategic significance at the entrance to the Bristol and English Channels. On the top of

Isles of Scilly

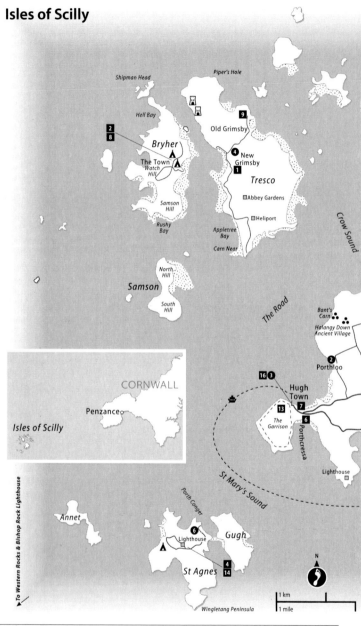

Shipman Head

Piper's Hole

Hell Bay

Old Grimsby

2
8

Bryher

4 New Grimsby

1

The Town
Watch Hill

Tresco

Samson Hill

Abbey Gardens

Rushy Bay

Heliport

Appletree Bay

Carn Near

North Hill

Samson

South Hill

Crow Sound

The Road

Bant's Carn

Halangy Down Ancient Village

Porthloo

2

16 **3**

Hugh Town

7

13

The Garrison

6

Porthcressa

St Mary's Sound

CORNWALL

Penzance○

Isles of Scilly

Lighthouse

To Western Rocks & Bishop Rock Lighthouse

Porth Conger

6
Lighthouse

Gugh

4
14

Annet

St Agnes

Wingletang Peninsula

N

1 km
1 mile

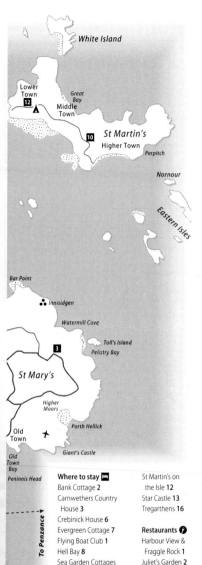

White Island

Lower Town 12

Great Bay

Middle Town

St Martin's 10

Higher Town

Perpitch

Nornour

Eastern Isles

Bar Point

Innisidgen

Watermill Cove

Toll's Island

Pelistry Bay 3

St Mary's

Higher Moors

Porth Hellick

Old Town

Giant's Castle

Old Town Bay

Peninnis Head

To Penzance

the low hill, approached through an impressive stone gateway, near the 18th-century **Rocket House**, which holds an exhibition on the Garrison's history, the granite bulk of **Star Castle** (now a hotel) was built for Elizabeth I in 1593, a pointed defence against the Spanish after the defeat of the Armada. Continuously fortified until the 20th century, the Garrison Walls and Civil War fortifications remain largely intact.

Heading the other way out of Hugh Town to the southeast leads up to the **Old Town** and **Peninnis Head**, with its lighthouse and strange weathered granite rocks, the Pulpit, Laughing Man and Tooth Rock. Overlooking **Old Town Bay**, the Old Church is a sacred old stone funeral chapel, candlelit only and surrounded by an evocative graveyard. One man was buried vertically here so he could go on looking out to sea. Beyond the airfield, civilization recedes as you approach **Porth Hellick**, site of Sir Cloudesley's grave and countless rock pools at low tide, past the **Giant's Castle rocks** and up to the passage graves and barrows on the Higher Moors. Further round the coast, beyond Pelistry Bay, a small sandy beach opposite Toll's Island, and Watermill Cove, are two well-preserved chambered tombs, at **Innisdgen**. Pointing north, **Bar Point** is one of the island of St Mary's most remote and peaceful beaches.

Continuing anti-clockwise round the island, **Halangy Down Ancient Village** is a pre-Celtic settlement overlooked by **Bant's Carn**, the most impressive of Scilly's chambered tombs, dating from 2000 BC. The coast path continues back to Hugh Town giving views across **The Road**, the stretch of water between St Mary's and Samson, Bryher and Tresco.

Tresco

Considerably smaller than St Mary's, 20 minutes across The Road by boat, Tresco is the most prettified and most famous of the Isles, thanks to its extraordinary subtropical Abbey Gardens laid out by Augustus Smith on south-facing terraces around his well-wooded Victorian manor house. The whole private island has a strange and slightly unreal atmosphere, being entirely dedicated to plant propagation and mild, polite holidaymaking. Like Portmeirion in Wales, with palm trees in place of eccentric Italian architecture, all the accommodation (including a good selection of self-catering cottages) on the island needs to be booked through the estate office. That said, the northern part of the island is as wild, rugged and lonely as anywhere in the Southwest, its heather and gorse dotted with barrows and chambered cairns.

At low tide, boats are forced to use the landing quay at Carn Near on the very southern tip, near Appletree Bay, a delightful beach of white sand so fine that it was once much in demand for blotting ink. Built around the ruins of a 12th-century priory, **Abbey Garden** ① *T01720-424105, www.tresco.co.uk, year round daily 1000-1600, £12, under-16s free,* supports an exotic and wonderfully varied range of plants, trees and shrubs; natives of Mexico, South Africa, the Canary Islands and Australasia in particular abound. Not too formally arranged, kind of Californian in style, the 12-acre gardens are full of surprises, not least the large collection of ships' figureheads rescued from wrecks in the Valhalla Museum near the entrance. The current lady of the manor has decorated a shell temple and Father Neptune sits imperiously at the top of the Lighthouse walk leading up the hill. There's also a wholesome café. A stunning coast road with views of Bryher over Appletree Bay runs along the west coast of the island to **New Grimsby**, Tresco's main harbour and settlement. On the coast to the north, Cromwell's and King Charles's ruined castles guard the channel between the two islands. At the harbour the road turns east over the back of Tresco, past the New Inn, the island's one and only pub, to the chic **Sea Garden Cottages at the Island Hotel**. Beyond these stylish one-bedroom cottages, a lonely track climbs into wilder countryside and back round to the castles. Halfway round, **Piper's Hole** is an impressive sea cave with an underground freshwater pool on the coast that can be reached on foot in less than an hour and explored with a torch.

Bryher and Samson

Just west of Tresco, separated by a tidal channel, Bryher is very different, the least domesticated of the inhabited islands, facing the full force of the Atlantic from the west. At its northern end, around Hell Bay, mountainous seas in gale force winds frequently overwhelm the spur of rock known as **Shipman Head**. The island's one settlement, called simply **The Town**, straggles along the eastern, Tresco side of **Watch Hill**, which true to its name gives glorious wraparound views across the entire archipelago. As well as its wild and broken west coast, Bryher has beautiful beaches on its southern shores, at Rushy Bay below Samson Hill, from where there are also extraordinary views in all directions and yet more lumpy tumuli in the rough grass. **Samson** itself, immediately due south, is the largest of the uninhabited islands. Its last 10 impoverished occupants underwent enforced evacuation by Augustus Smith in the mid-19th century, the remains of their village and industry still visible today on South Hill. Both North and South Hills, separated by a low sandy isthmus, are also topped with chambered cairns.

St Martin's

Many visitors' favourite island, but still unlikely to be at all crowded, St Martin's lies north of St Mary's beyond Crow Sound, in the comparative shelter afforded by Tresco, Bryher and Samson to its west. A ridge of granite, the northern coast is rugged, with the exception of **Great Bay**'s sandy beach, one of the widest and most remote in Scilly. Beyond Great Bay, a tidal causeway links the northwest of the island with lonely and mysterious **White Island**. The southern side has more superb beaches, especially **Par**, **Perpitch** and **Lower Town**, and is lined with flower farms along the mile-long road between Lower Town and Higher Town.

St Agnes

The smallest, most southerly and most independent of the inhabited islands, separated from the others by the deep water channel of St Mary's Sound, St Agnes is like a child's drawing of an island. A little white lighthouse, one of the oldest in the country, stands proudly in the middle, surrounded by a wonderful array of places to explore: sandy beaches, coves, tidal islands, high-hedged little flower farms, an ancient stone maze, a mysterious well, and strange rock formations among other things. Boats land at Porth Conger, in the north of the island, near the only pub, **The Turk's Head**. A single track road then climbs up to the hill to the lighthouse (disused), passing a small turning on the left leading to the tidal sand bar connecting St Agnes to Gugh, with its megalithic remains and weather-beaten castles of rock. **Beady Pool** on the remote Wingletang Peninsula gets its name from small Spanish glass balls still very occasionally found here over 200 years after the ship carrying them went down just offshore.

Isles of Scilly listings

For hotel and restaurant price codes and other relevant information, see pages 9-13.

Where to stay

Note that most accommodation on Scilly needs to be booked well in advance, especially in high season.

St Mary's p85

££££-£££ Star Castle Hotel, The Garrison, St Mary's, T01720-422317, star-castle.co.uk. 16th-century castle in the shape of an 8-point star, 38 bedrooms and suites in the castle and garden, many with superb sea views. A 13-m-long indoor pool is on site, with horse riding, tennis courts, golf and boat trips available nearby.

££££-£££ Tregarthens, close to the quay, T01720-422540, www.tregarthens-hotel.co.uk. The island's oldest hotel (dating from 1848), with 33 luxurious en suite bedrooms, many with views across the harbour.

£££ Carnwethers Country House, Pelistry Bay, T01720-422415, www.carnwethers.com. Out of the thick of things, a mile and a half from Hugh Town on the other side of the island, comprising 4 self-catering apartments set in attractive grounds of an acre. Solar-heated saline outdoor pool and games room.

£££-££ Crebinick House, Church St, Hugh Town, T01720-422968, www.crebinick.co.uk. Comfortable B&B in a granite cottage.

££ Evergreen Cottage, Parade, in Hugh Town, T01720-422711, www.evergreen cottageguesthouse.co.uk. Another cosy guesthouse, set in a lovely garden.

Tresco p88

££££ Sea Garden Cottages at the Island Hotel, Tresco, T01720-422849, www.tresco.co.uk. Luxury 1-bedroom contemporary cottages with balconies or terraces overlooking the beach. Facilities include tennis courts, heated indoor swimming pool, gym, jacuzzi and sauna.

£££ Flying Boat Club, Tresco, T01720-422849, www.tresco.co.uk. 12 luxury beachfront houses sleeping up to 12, access to the **Flying Boat Restaurant** and **Tresco Spa**. See also Restaurants below.

Bryher p88

££££-£££ Hell Bay Hotel, T01720-422947, www.hellbay.co.uk. 25 beautiful suites with Lloyd Loom furniture, Malabar fabrics and paintings by Cornwall's leading artists. Wonderful, remote bolthole.

£££ Bank Cottage, T01720-422612, www.bank-cottage.com. Guesthouse with 3 twins and 1 double, plus a self-catering cottage.

£££-££ Harbour View and Fraggle Rock, T01720-422222, www.bryher.co. The island's pub, which also has accommodation.

Camping

Bryher Campsite T01720-422559, www.bryhercampsite.co.uk. Spectacularly positioned with views of the harbour and neighbouring Tresco.

St Martin's p89

£££ Polreath, T01720-422046, www.polreath.com, 4 bedrooms in a little cottage near the quay, it's the most famous B&B on the island and also runs the tearooms.

Camping

St Martin's Campsite, Oakland's Farm, Middle Town, T01720-422888, www.stmartinscampsite.co.uk. Sheltered behind hedges, right on a glorious bay. Booking in advance inthe summer.

St Agnes *p89*

£££ The Parsonage, T01720-422370, next to the lightouse, offers self-catering accommodation in flats and a barn, set in attractive gardens.

£££ St Agnes Lighthouse Farm Holiday Lets, T01720-422514, lighthousefarm@stagnesscilly.co.uk, or book via www.scillyonline.co.uk. Self-catering accommodation with a choice of 3 properties around the lighthouse.

Camping

Troytown Farm Campsite Troy Town Farm, T01720-422360, www.troytown.co.uk. Stunning location facing the Atlantic with views of Bishop Rock Lighthouse and Western Rocks, homemade ice cream and other farm-fresh goodies. Also has self-catering accommodation. Book well in advance for the summer months.

Restaurants

St Mary's *p85*

££ Juliet's Garden, Seaways Flower Farm, Porthloo, T01720-422228, www.juliets gardenrestaurant.co.uk. Mar-Oct daily 1000 and in the evenings Tue-Sun high season. A 20-min walk from Hugh Town, with superb views from its balcony room and terrace, a good place to enjoy a very fine crab salad or cream tea and one of the best restaurants on St Mary's. Evening menu specializes in steaks and fresh seafood.

££ Mermaid Inn, T01720-422701, overlooking the harbour in Hugh Town. Strewn with smugglers' loot and wreckage and evening meals feature freshly caught fish.

Tresco *p88*

££ The New Inn, New Grimsby, T01720-422844. The island's pub, open all year, nautical memorabilia, excellent food and fine ales, simple, comfortable bedrooms.

St Agnes *p89*

££-£ Turk's Head Pub, T01720-422434. Famous Island pasties, crab sandwiches and very good real ale.

Festivals

Isles of Scilly *p84*

Gig racing is the big spectator sport in the Scilly Isles, when locals compete to row their old pilot boats from Nut Point to St Mary's as quickly as possible, a reminder of the days when first on won the contract, sometimes to take ships as far as Liverpool.

May The World Pilot Gig Championships, www.worldgigs.co.uk, take place in the first May Day Bank Holiday. Throughout the season, Wed nights the women race, Fri the men.

What to do

Isles of Scilly *p84*
Boat trips and watersports
Island Sea Safaris, T01720-422732, www.islandseasafaris.co.uk. Wildlife-watching trips aboard a high-speed RIB, visiting seal colonies and snorkelling.

St Martin's Dive School, Highertown, St Martin's, T01720-422848, www.scillydiving.com. Dive school, snorkelling with seals.

The Sailing Centre, Porthmellon, St Mary's, T01720-424919, www.sailingscilly.com. Windsurfing and dinghy sailing lessons, sea kayak hire.

Boat trips are also offered by: **Blue Hunter**, T01720-423377; **Calypso**, T01720-422187 and **Crusader**, T01720-243122.

Horse riding
St Mary's Riding Centre, T01720-423855, www.horsesonscilly.co.uk. Explore the bridleways, beaches and farm tracks around the east coast.

Island tours

Island Rover, T01720-422131. Open-top bus tours round St Mary's with enlightening commentary. Mon-Sat from Hugh Town.
Island Wildlife Tours, T01720-422212. Birdwatching tours with local expert Will Wagstaff.

⊖ Transport

St Mary's *p85*
Bicycle
St Mary's Bike Hire, The Strand, Hugh Town, St Mary's, T01720-422289. Mon-Sat 0900-1700. Bike hire on Tresco T01720-422849.

Taxi
St Mary's Taxis, T01720-422555.

❶ Directory

Isles of Scilly *p84*
Medical facilities Doctor T01720-422628; dentist, T01720-422694. The only chemist on the islands is **R Douglas** at The Bank, Hugh Town, St Mary's, T01720-422403.

Contents

Footnotes

Index

Titles available in the Footprint *Focus* range

Latin America	UK RRP	US RRP
Bahia & Salvador	£7.99	$11.95
Brazilian Amazon	£7.99	$11.95
Brazilian Pantanal	£6.99	$9.95
Buenos Aires & Pampas	£7.99	$11.95
Cartagena & Caribbean Coast	£7.99	$11.95
Costa Rica	£8.99	$12.95
Cuzco, La Paz & Lake Titicaca	£8.99	$12.95
El Salvador	£5.99	$8.95
Guadalajara & Pacific Coast	£6.99	$9.95
Guatemala	£8.99	$12.95
Guyana, Guyane & Suriname	£5.99	$8.95
Havana	£6.99	$9.95
Honduras	£7.99	$11.95
Nicaragua	£7.99	$11.95
Northeast Argentina & Uruguay	£8.99	$12.95
Paraguay	£5.99	$8.95
Quito & Galápagos Islands	£7.99	$11.95
Recife & Northeast Brazil	£7.99	$11.95
Rio de Janeiro	£8.99	$12.95
São Paulo	£5.99	$8.95
Uruguay	£6.99	$9.95
Venezuela	£8.99	$12.95
Yucatán Peninsula	£6.99	$9.95

Asia	UK RRP	US RRP
Angkor Wat	£5.99	$8.95
Bali & Lombok	£8.99	$12.95
Chennai & Tamil Nadu	£8.99	$12.95
Chiang Mai & Northern Thailand	£7.99	$11.95
Goa	£6.99	$9.95
Gulf of Thailand	£8.99	$12.95
Hanoi & Northern Vietnam	£8.99	$12.95
Ho Chi Minh City & Mekong Delta	£7.99	$11.95
Java	£7.99	$11.95
Kerala	£7.99	$11.95
Kolkata & West Bengal	£5.99	$8.95
Mumbai & Gujarat	£8.99	$12.95

For the latest books, e-books and a wealth of travel information, visit us at: www.footprinttravelguides.com.

 footprinttravelguides.com

Africa & Middle East	UK RRP	US RRP
Beirut	£6.99	$9.95
Cairo & Nile Delta	£8.99	$12.95
Damascus	£5.99	$8.95
Durban & KwaZulu Natal	£8.99	$12.95
Fès & Northern Morocco	£8.99	$12.95
Jerusalem	£8.99	$12.95
Johannesburg & Kruger National Park	£7.99	$11.95
Kenya's Beaches	£8.99	$12.95
Kilimanjaro & Northern Tanzania	£8.99	$12.95
Luxor to Aswan	£8.99	$12.95
Nairobi & Rift Valley	£7.99	$11.95
Red Sea & Sinai	£7.99	$11.95
Zanzibar & Pemba	£7.99	$11.95

Europe	UK RRP	US RRP
Bilbao & Basque Region	£6.99	$9.95
Brittany West Coast	£7.99	$11.95
Cádiz & Costa de la Luz	£6.99	$9.95
Granada & Sierra Nevada	£6.99	$9.95
Languedoc: Carcassonne to Montpellier	£7.99	$11.95
Málaga	£5.99	$8.95
Marseille & Western Provence	£7.99	$11.95
Orkney & Shetland Islands	£5.99	$8.95
Santander & Picos de Europa	£7.99	$11.95
Sardinia: Alghero & the North	£7.99	$11.95
Sardinia: Cagliari & the South	£7.99	$11.95
Seville	£5.99	$8.95
Sicily: Palermo & the Northwest	£7.99	$11.95
Sicily: Catania & the Southeast	£7.99	$11.95
Siena & Southern Tuscany	£7.99	$11.95
Sorrento, Capri & Amalfi Coast	£6.99	$9.95
Skye & Outer Hebrides	£6.99	$9.95
Verona & Lake Garda	£7.99	$11.95

North America	UK RRP	US RRP
Vancouver & Rockies	£8.99	$12.95

Australasia	UK RRP	US RRP
Brisbane & Queensland	£8.99	$12.95
Perth	£7.99	$11.95

 Join us on facebook for the latest travel news, product releases, offers and amazing competitions: www.facebook.com/footprintbooks.